HOW TO CREATE WEALTH BY INVESTING IN STOCKS

WEALTHY

&

WISE

DAVID CHENIER

2024 EDITION

WEALTHY & WISE

ISBN: 978-1-7377116-7-4

Cover Design: Stephanie Dubois
Interior Formatting: Nonon Tech & Design
Editor: Michelle Gean

Disclaimer/legal

Please read this before reading the book.

All information in this book is for educational and informational purposes ONLY. Should you decide to take any action as a result of this book, you do so at your own risk. You should not construe any information or other material as investment, tax, legal, financial, or any other advice. Past performance does not indicate future results. You are fully responsible for any decisions you make, as all information provided by David Chenier is for educational purposes only. You should do your own due diligence and research this book's topics yourself before making any decisions.

Warren Buffett and Charlie Munger were already wealthy and wise when I became aware of them almost 40 years ago, and I have been inspired by how they think, communicate, and behave ever since. I am grateful to them both.

TABLE OF CONTENTS

INTRODUCTION

Money can be a complicated topic because it is deeply personal for most of us. We usually do not talk about it with others, and if we are lucky enough to have family and friends who will talk about it with us, we often do not talk about it deeply enough or in a way that allows us to make actionable changes in our savings and investing habits.

Unfortunately, when we look beyond those closest to us, there are not many "financial helpers" (or resources) you can trust with your money management. Most financial helpers are trained in selling, not in investing, and often their focus is on how to make profits for themselves—not for you. Even if they are skilled enough within the realm of investing, when helpers profit off of you, they will be incentivized to ensure you cannot do it by yourself, and they may make it intentionally more complicated than it needs to be. So, much of what I want to cover here is not available from third-party resources nor is it taught in schools.

The inaugural, 2022 edition of this book was written as a private document for my family and a few friends. When I was just starting to invest, it was much more difficult than I think it should've been. I was frustrated, and still am, by the lack of clear, objective information and the dearth of capable resources. So much so that I decided to write what I wished I could've read when I was starting to learn about stock investing, decades ago. I had no financial motives for writing the 2022 edition. I simply believe creating wealth is an important discussion to have in a safe setting with family and close friends, and my hope was that what I wrote would be useful in those discussions.

After writing the first edition of *Wealthy & Wise*, I was surprised to learn that my approach to stock investing was different from my family and friend's; my methodology was simple, yet it outperformed. Based on the feedback from family and friends, I decided to update the content and share the information more broadly, which is the copy you are holding today. The content has some partial information about my savings that I would have preferred not to share. I thought about removing the numbers, but you need them to understand the material.

With this context shared, let's begin.

THE POWER OF
INVESTING

"I made my first investment at age eleven.

I was wasting my life up until then."

— WARREN BUFFETT

I bought my first stocks in 1985, and for the first seven years, my investing results were not memorable. I was lost in a storm. I traded too frequently, looked to the market for the "Truth," and listened to market helpers (analysts, brokers, and financial media) as though they were high priests who could help me understand the market's mysteries.

I first became aware of Warren Buffett in the middle of that storm. The unique clarity of Warren's communications and his humor captivated me. The clouds began to disperse. I eagerly began reading and listening to anything with or about Buffett (and still do). I became aware of Charlie Munger because of Warren. The sun came out over my investments and the storm ended. These two generous, capable, witty guides would help me figure out where I wanted to go and how to get there when it came to investing.

I learn best by doing. I bought my first share of Berkshire Hathaway in 1993, and it was the investment in Berkshire Hathaway (and learning from Warren Buffett's and Charlie Munger's communications over the years) that improved my stock investing results. I make investing mistakes, plenty of mistakes, but I have been able to create wealth by investing in stocks with overall good results, beating both the market and my expectations.

Photo of Warren Buffett and David Chenier in 2000
(I met Warren, quite a highlight for me, but we do not know each other.)

When stock investing is done rationally and over a long period of time, you can create wealth. You do not need an expensive financial degree or a high level of formal intelligence to do this. What you need are some behavioral habits that allow you to harness the power of compound interest over long time periods. Some of the behavioral habits you may already possess. Others you can learn or further develop over time while building your wealth. Many skills diminish with age, but investing can be different. The experience you gain, if you have the courage to expose yourself to investing, and the capital you can accumulate over the years can allow you, the investor, to improve with age. But first you must start, and as you will see, the earlier you start the better.

You will also discover that investing with the *Wealthy & Wise* methodology will be about much more than just making money. The successful investor develops an ability to think independently, and their investing activities provide incentives and countless opportunities to enhance their mental powers of reason, imagination, and empathy—traits crucial to a person's overall wellbeing. You will gain a deeper understanding of the human condition, the state of the world, and transformative ideas that can make you both wealthy and wise—plus investing can be a lot of fun.

When you invest in stocks the Wealthy & Wise way, you are investing in businesses. One of the many things I have learned is that good businesses are rare and special. A successful stock investor becomes a collector—collecting good businesses by owning shares of stock—who is curious about, and paying attention to, the underlying businesses.

Have you ever noticed that almost every type of collector is happy? I have. Think about it. How many unhappy collectors do you know? There is just something in the human condition that makes collectors happy humans. So, why not be a collector and collect good businesses? You will learn a lot about the businesses, obviously, but also about impactful ideas that involve yourself, humanity, and the world.

Happy, Wealthy, and Wise is not a bad outcome in life, and it's not too late.

We will start by looking at the magic of compounding, the importance of beginning to invest as early as possible, and the benefits of investing in stocks of individual businesses instead of mutual funds. The advantages of investing in the stocks of individual good businesses (over mutual funds) and holding them for decades, for as long as they remain good businesses, are numerous and significant, and too many people are kept unaware of the benefits. Actual compounding results from real-world investments will be used to introduce the key elements of a buy-and-hold stock investing methodology.

It will be the quality of the underlying business that you invest in which determines your returns when shares of stock are held for decades. We will look at how you can select stocks of high-quality businesses for long-term investments, including how to assess the value of the underlying business and how to take advantage of stock market volatility. If you buy-and-hold a diversified collection of stocks in good to wonderful businesses, you really should not lose money overall if the stocks are held long enough (held for decades). Your long-term, buy-and-hold winners with ending values that are up ten, twenty, forty, or more, times their beginning values should more than pay for the number of losers you can reasonably expect to own in your collection.

Those sections will help you create wealth by investing in stocks. Once you have accumulated some wealth, the final section will outline how you can create high levels of income and further enhance your overall investing results by selling stock options with the stocks that you already own, or want to own, within your collection of buy-and-hold investments.

The world of stock options can be risky and complex, but the options section in this book will walk you through a well-defined strategy for selling options that is simple, does not take much time, has relatively low risks, and importantly, it does all of that without you having to be able to predict near-term stock price movements. When you utilize the recommended options strategy, named SUPER-CPT, it will greatly reduce the complex and risky options world to a simpler, safer subset of option trading activities. For such a low-risk strategy, SUPER-CPT can be very lucrative. Instead of having gains only in an up stock market, you can generate income no matter which way the stock price trends (down, sideways, or up), and when combined with a buy-and-hold stock investing methodology, it can be more financially rewarding than if you only do buy-and-hold stock investing. When selling options with the recommended strategy, the cumulative net premiums you can earn are more than you probably imagine. Actual results from selling options over an extended period are included so that you can reach your own conclusions.

The behavioral aspects of successful investing are crucial and will be covered throughout the book and summarized at the end. Investing with the Wealthy & Wise methodology is not a get-rich-quick scheme. Often, the road to quick wealth leads to quickly becoming broke. Everything discussed here is a relatively low-risk approach to making the most out of your money.

A summary and suggestions to tilt the odds of success in your favor will be included at the end of each major section.

"THE SECRET TO YOUR FINANCIAL SUCCESS IS INSIDE
YOURSELF. IF YOU BECOME A CRITICAL THINKER WHO
TAKES NO WALL STREET 'FACT' ON FAITH, AND YOU
INVEST WITH PATIENT CONFIDENCE, YOU CAN TAKE
STEADY ADVANTAGE OF EVEN THE WORST BEAR
MARKETS. BY DEVELOPING YOUR DISCIPLINE AND
COURAGE, YOU CAN REFUSE TO LET OTHER PEOPLE'S
MOOD SWINGS GOVERN YOUR FINANCIAL DESTINY.
IN THE END, HOW YOUR INVESTMENTS BEHAVE IS
MUCH LESS IMPORTANT THAN HOW YOU BEHAVE."

— Ben Graham

THE MAGIC OF COMPOUNDING

When I was young, I enjoyed reading stories about ordinary people (schoolteachers, janitors, barbers, and so on) holding stocks in a company, or a few companies, for long periods of time. Their steadfastness resulted in large sums of money as the values of the stocks they held increased. I observed that those financial gains gave them independence while also enhancing their ability to make positive impacts in the world around them. Witnessing how anyone could get rich with a little patience and informed choice was what motivated me to start investing. I wanted to do that.

A key enabler of getting rich in these instances was time: the sooner you save and invest, even if it is only small amounts, more time will be available for compounding to occur and create wealth. More time gives you a huge edge. Time allows the "magic of compounding" to transform small sums of money into large amounts, because compounding creates exponential growth. Exponential growth is repeated multiplication at each interval whereas linear growth is simply addition at each interval. For example, linear growth is 30+30=60, while exponential growth is 30*30=900. The difference in growth is huge. Exponential growth is common in nature, but the human mind struggles to grasp the effects of exponential growth after many intervals. Compounding results over extended periods are simply not naturally intuitive. Compounding outcomes from repeated intervals are incredible, astonishing, and even magical. When you truly understand compound interest, your entire perspective on investing will change.

"Compound interest is the eighth wonder of the world."
— ALBERT EINSTEIN

The growth from compounding will appear slow at first, when the values are small, but the amounts really ramp up in the later periods with startling effects. As an example, and it is one that is widely used, if you were offered the choice between an immediate cash payment of one million dollars or a magic penny that doubled every day until day 30, which one would you take? At first, you might jump on the million-dollar deal. But if you accept one penny that doubles each day until day 30, (a penny on day one, two pennies on day two, four pennies on day three, and so on for thirty days), on day 30 your penny would be worth over $5,000,000 (refer to the table below).

A Magic Penny That Doubles Every Day
Will Be Over $5 million In 30 Days

1	$0.01	11	$10.24	21	$10,485.76
2	$0.02	12	$20.48	22	$20,971.52
3	$0.04	13	$40.96	23	$41,943.04
4	$0.08	14	$81.92	24	$83,886.08
5	$0.16	15	$163.84	25	$167,772.16
6	$0.32	16	$327.68	26	$335,544.32
7	$0.64	17	$655.36	27	$671,088.64
8	$1.28	18	$1,310.72	28	$1,342,177.28
9	$2.56	19	$2,621.44	29	$2,684,354.56
10	$5.12	20	$5,242.88	30	$5,368,709.12

Because compounding has such a huge impact on the outcome of money in the later years, it is crucial that you start investing early in life: now.

Compounding goes slow until it goes fast. As you test this equation, you will see that even on day 20 your penny is only worth about $5,000. The magic occurs in the later years when the compounding is being applied to increasingly larger numbers. On day 10, you are doubling $5; on day 20, you're doubling $5,000; on the second to last day, you're doubling $2,500,000.

Now, just for fun, inject yourself into the magic penny example. Instead of the amounts doubling per day, imagine each amount doubling over the period of a year, and liken the 30 days to the 30 years you are in the workforce with the option to put money aside for retirement.

Now imagine that, for whatever reason, for the first 10 years you decide you do not need to worry about retirement or can't afford to put anything aside, or whatever other excuse you might come up with. In the above example, that means you would only have had 20 compounding periods instead of 30, and your penny would have been worth only $5,243 instead of $5,368,709 in the end. Startling and accurate!

So, if you are telling yourself now that you will put aside money for tomorrow "when you can afford to" or "when you make more money" or whatever, you are putting yourself at a huge disadvantage. Regardless of how much you make, the sooner you get started, the sooner the 8th wonder of the world will start working for you. Even a very small amount of money saved when you are very young could mean many millions in retirement.

Exponential growth is magical, and even better, it really exists. When you imagine doubling an amount every year that is a compound annual growth rate of 100%. Doubling every day, or even every year, is a useful illustrative example, but it is an unrealistically high annual growth rate to expect from personal investments over many years. Realistic growth rates, over an extended period (decades), from actual investments will be much lower but can still be satisfactory. Let's look at real-life examples, starting with an actual investment portfolio.

COMPOUNDING RESULTS FROM AN ACTUAL INVESTMENT PORTFOLIO

My work career started in 1985 when I was 23 years old. I began contributing to a retirement savings account (often referred to as a 401-K) at my first employer. When I quit in 1990 to take a job at another company, I moved a portion of the retirement savings account to a stockbroker and opened an Individual Retirement Account (IRA), a tax-deferred account that enables you to defer paying taxes on income contributed and any investment gains until you are 72 years old. I could have rolled all my 401-K retirement savings into my new company's 401-K plan, but I wanted to have more money to invest in individual stock names instead of just the mutual funds and employer's stock that were offered in the new employer's plan.

The IRA account's value was $27,000 on January 1, 1992. I had other accounts and added new money to those over the years, but I never added money to, nor withdrew any money from, the IRA account from January 1, 1992 through March 31, 2021. Therefore, any growth in the account value over those 29 years, from January 1, 1992, through March 31, 2021, was solely the result of the growth in the stock values held in the account. I added new money to the IRA account when I retired in May 2021 and consolidated accounts, but that was after and it had no impact on the March 31, 2021, ending value. During those 29 years, I made lots of mistakes and would do some things differently, with hindsight, but the IRA account will provide a real-world example of exponential growth that is more realistic than the magic penny example.

COMPOUNDING CAN CREATE MORE THAN 98% OF AN ACTUAL RETIREMENT ACCOUNT

That same IRA account with a beginning value of $27,000 was valued at $1.6 million on March 31, 2021, with no money added, nor withdrawn, during those twenty-nine years (refer to the graph below). The ending value of $1.6 million is 59 times larger than the beginning value (1,600,000 divided by 27,000 equals 59).

15% Compound Annual Growth Rate
Beginning Value of $27,000 followed by no deposits nor withdrawals for 29 years

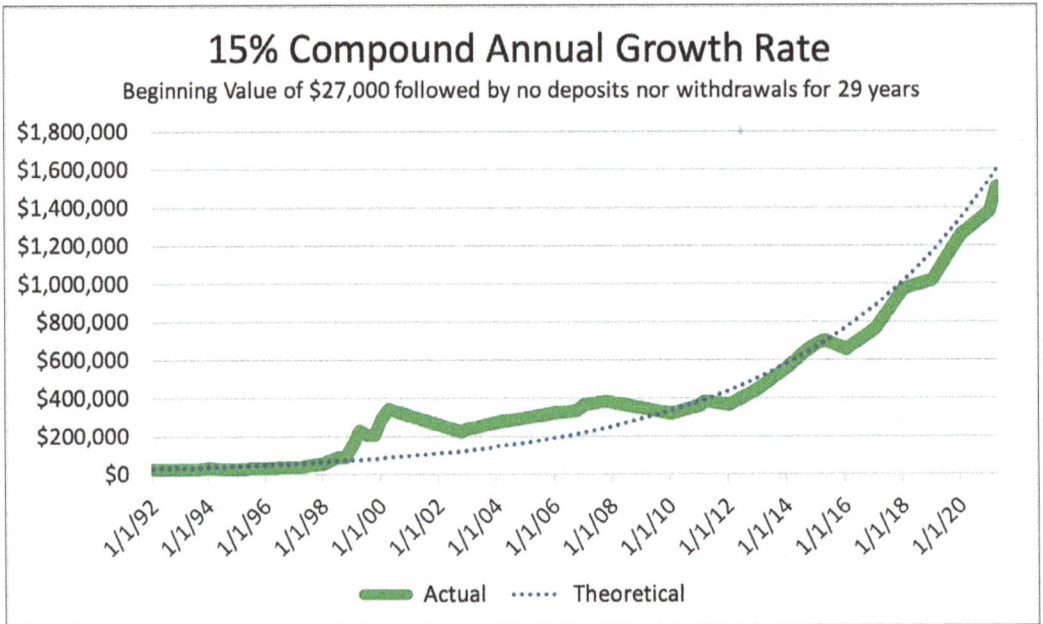

Legend: Actual, Theoretical

You must invest your savings as early as you can. The longer you wait, the more you will have to save to reach a wealth goal. In the actual example, only $27,000 had to be saved to reach $1.6 million in 29 years. The amount of savings in the IRA ($27,000) is less than 2% of the $1.6 million (27,000 divided by 1,600,000 equals 1.7%). The rest of the IRA account, more than 98%, was created through the magic of compounding over a 29-year period.

Without investing, if you want to reach $1.6 million in 29 years you need to save $1.6 million, equivalent to setting aside $55,000 each year for 29 years.

> *"All the math you need in the stock market*
> *you get in the fourth grade."*
> — PETER LYNCH

When you truly understand compound interest, your entire perspective on investing changes, but to gain that understanding, it requires you to do a little bit of math. There is no need to stress out. Please do not stop reading here; you do not need to know a lot of math and what you need to know does not get more complex or change over time, so it will become simple once you make the effort to use it regularly.

The math that you will need to know is Compound Annual Growth Rate (CAGR). CAGR is used to calculate the average annual growth rate of an investment over a specific period. It is the rate of return that would be required for an investment to grow from its beginning value to its ending value, assuming the profits remained reinvested at the end of each year of the investment's lifespan. You should use compound annual growth rate to compare two or more alternative investments and to estimate future values.

The IRA account's value grew at a compound annual growth rate of 15% during those twenty-nine years; said another way, a beginning value of $27,000 multiplied by 1.15 twenty-nine times is equal to a $1.6 million ending value. When something grows 15% on average each year that is an exponential function. Mathematically, the growth in the IRA account is equivalent to $27{,}000 \times (1.15^{29}) = 1.6$ million. The number of years, 29, is the exponent.

Now, here is how you can calculate the compound annual growth rate when all you know is the beginning value, ending value, and the number of years. This tiny bit of math is very useful in investing; it will not be difficult once you start to use it regularly and there will be no more additional math needed once you learn this. Below are the steps, from Investopedia.com, for how to calculate a compound annual growth rate (CAGR) using the IRA account's numbers.

1. Divide the value of an investment at the end of the period by its value at the beginning of that period: for the IRA account, the formula would yield 59 (1,600,000 divided by 27,000).

2. Raise the result to an exponent of one divided by the number of years: for the account, this formula would yield 1.15 ($59^{(1/29)}$).

3. Subtract one from the prior result: for the account, this would equate to be 0.15 (1.15 minus 1).

4. Multiply by 100 to convert the answer into a percentage: for the account, this would be 15% (0.15 multiplied by 100).

Alternatively, the formula to use in a Microsoft Excel spreadsheet when the CAGR cell is formatted as a percentage would be:

CAGR = (Ending Value/Beginning Value)^(1/Number of Years) – 1

The IRA account's CAGR using the Excel formula would be as follows: CAGR = $(1,600,000/27,000)^{(1/29)}$-1 = 15% CAGR. Whether you use Excel or the methodology from Investopedia, the answer is the same: the compound annual growth rate (CAGR)—when the IRA investment portfolio grew by 59 times in 29 years, from $27,000 in 1992 to $1,600,000 in 2021—is 15%.

That is the end of the math exercise. I am imagining some of you cheering as I put away the dentist drill.

The actual IRA account's growth rate of 15% is a much lower rate than the magic penny that doubles every day or every year (100% CAGR), but a 15% CAGR is a very satisfactory growth rate to achieve in the real world of investing.

The Standard and Poor's 500, or simply the S&P 500, is a stock market index that tracks the stock performance of 500 of the largest companies listed in the US. The S&P 500 acts as a benchmark for the performance of the US stock market overall. A rough rule of thumb is that compound annual growth rates over the long-term in the US have averaged about 10% for the stock market (stocks), 4-5% for fixed income (bonds and US Treasury Bills), and 3% for inflation. Importantly, the rates are historical averages over the long-term. Rates were much more variable over short time periods, especially in the stock market. These rates are also not adjusted for inflation. 'Nominal' rates of return are not adjusted for inflation, while 'real' rates are.

Even small differences in compound annual growth rates over long periods of time will create vastly different results (refer to the graph below). When $27,000 grew at a 15% compound annual growth rate, it became $1.6 million, a value 59 times larger than the original $27,000 that was invested 29 years prior. If $27,000 grew at a 10% compound annual growth rate for 29 years, it only becomes $400,000. At a 5% compound annual growth rate, that same value only becomes $100,000 after 29 years.

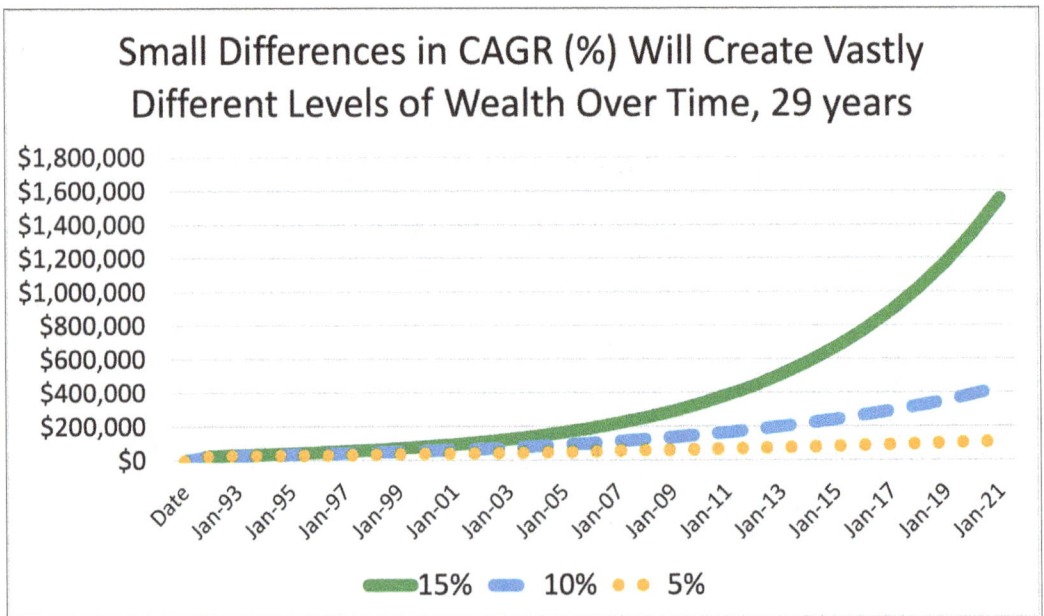

Different CAGRS yield significantly different wealth outcomes. The magic occurs in the later years when the compounding is being applied to increasingly larger numbers; these compounding results over the long-term (decades) are not naturally intuitive. If they were, young people would be much more motivated to save and start investing earlier. The wealth differences shown on the graph only capture 29 years; the differences in wealth will expand even more over time.

More time will allow more compounding, creating much more wealth for a given growth rate (refer to the graph below). Withdrawals do not need to start from the IRA account until 2034, allowing 42 years of compounding after the beginning value of $27,000 was deposited in 1992. At 42 years and a 15% growth rate, your $27,000 of savings would grow to above $9.5 million, but with a 5% growth rate, after 42 years, you would only be at $200,000. Savings of $27,000 multiplied by 1.15 forty-two times (1.15^{42}) grows into a vastly different level of wealth than when it is multiplied by 1.05 forty-two times (1.05^{42}).

The hugely different wealth outcomes illustrate why it is useful to learn, as early as you can, how to increase the compound annual growth rates that you can achieve with your investments. You can, and should, use compound annual growth rates to evaluate how different investments have performed over time or against a benchmark, like the S&P 500. I invested the $27,000 in individual stocks (businesses), but I could have invested it in an index mutual fund that tracks the overall stock market, which grew historically on average at a 10% CAGR (before fees and taxes), or I could have put the money into fixed income investments that grew historically at less than a 5% CAGR. The IRA account's actual 15% CAGR is 50% better than the stock market's long-term average, but the outcome in dollars is 400% better, at $1.6 million versus only $0.4 million. The relative difference will continue to grow over time.

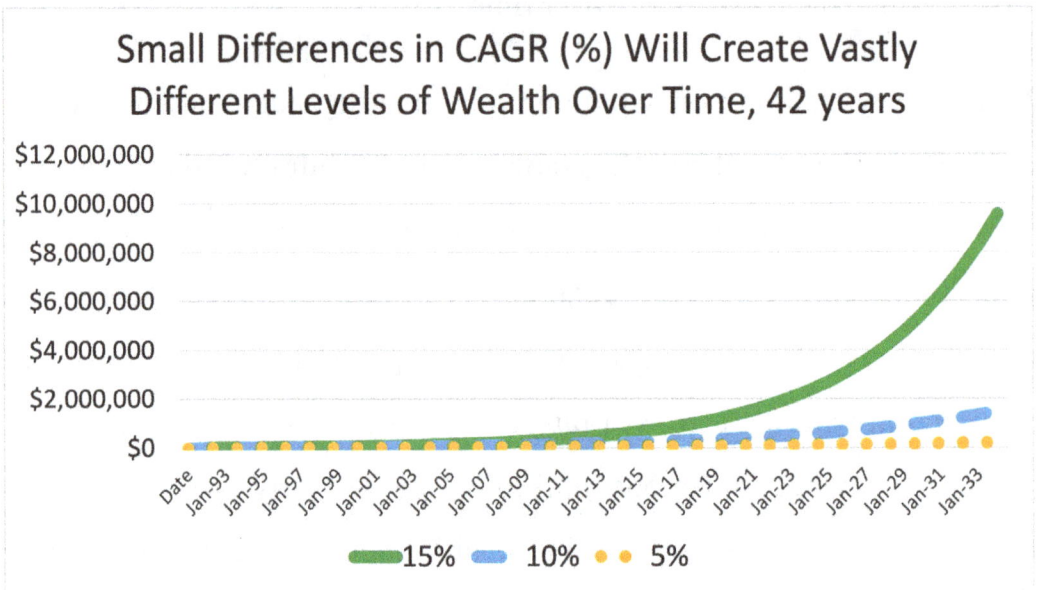

Your investments do not have to have a CAGR greater than the market to create wealth. Your investments only need to beat inflation to create real wealth. The rates being used are not adjusted for inflation. If you assume the rule of thumb of 3% inflation, $27,000 in 1992 is equivalent to $64,000 in 2021. (It is the same formula, 27,000 multiplied by 1.03 twenty-nine times equals 64,000.) Inflation will barely dent an IRA account that grew at 15% CAGR, $1.6 million is so much more than $64,000. However, inflation takes a very large percentage toll on your wealth with lower growth rates, and if you earn less than 3% CAGR on your investments your real wealth, after adjusting for inflation, will be declining. Keeping your savings in cash, earning no interest, or even putting it into a savings account earning less than 3% interest per year will steadily erode your real wealth, once adjusted for inflation. Many people think holding cash has no risk, but over the long-term, it does have risk since the real value of the cash held will decline steadily at the inflation rate each year.

Hopefully, you would agree that the IRA account is a simple, real-life example of how investing can unleash compounding to create wealth over time. I had other investment accounts at the same time as the IRA. The IRA account was not the best performing account, but it is the simplest to explain. I added new money on a regular basis to the other accounts; those inflows, and some outflows, of funds complicate an explanation of CAGR for those accounts, but a similar beneficial compounding effect has happened to each of my stock investment accounts over time.

BUY-AND-HOLD STOCK INVESTING METHODOLOGY

When you purchase stocks of publicly traded businesses, if the businesses continue to perform well, you should ignore the stock price and just hold onto your shares. Holding is much harder to do than it sounds, a bit like dieting. Easy to understand (move more, eat less) but difficult for many people to do. Stock prices can be very volatile, constantly moving up and down erratically, but over long time periods (years), stock prices will generally follow the underlying business's performance, good or bad. If the businesses do well, the stocks in your portfolio will do well and vice versa.

The stock market was volatile, with lots of ups and downs, during the IRA account's 29-year period. A 5-year period, 1995 – 2000, became known as the dot.com bubble and then the market crashed in the spring of 2000. The values in the investment accounts rose before they crashed, and the values were overall lower than the prior highs for almost 4 years before starting to climb upwards again beyond 2005. That cycle has repeated itself a few times since then.

But timing the market is not the path to success—no one can predict when a boom or crash will happen. Stocks move in fits and starts. A year's worth of gains can be won in just a few days, or missed if you just so happen to be out of the market on those days. You cannot predict when those big days, weeks, or months will happen. No one has ever done so reliably. You need to already be in the market when the booms begin. The money saved and invested prior to 1995 enabled the investment portfolio to fully benefit from the 1995-2000 boom period.

A key rationale for buy-and-hold investing is that you will make far more money by holding through bull markets (booms) than you lose by holding through bear markets (crashes). That rationale is what happened during the dot.com boom and bust. The IRA account gained much more during the dot.com boom than was lost in the crash that followed, and that has happened consistently during other boom and bust cycles. The same rationale played out in each of the other investment accounts and with individual stock names as well.

> *"Far more money has been lost by investors trying to anticipate corrections, than lost in the corrections themselves."*
> — PETER LYNCH

Benjamin Graham in his classic 1949 book, *The Intelligent Investor*, tells a relevant story below:

"Back in the spring of 1720, Sir Isaac Newton owned shares in the South Sea Company, the hottest stock in England. Sensing that the market was getting out of hand, the great physicist muttered that he 'could calculate the motions of the heavenly bodies, but not the madness of the people.' Newton dumped his South Sea shares, pocketing a 100% profit totaling £7,000. But just months later, swept up in the wild enthusiasm of the market, Newton jumped back in at a much higher price — and lost £20,000 (or more than $5 million in today's money). For the rest of his life, he forbade anyone to speak the words 'South Sea' in his presence."

The protagonist in Ben Graham's story, Sir Isaac Newton, is one of the greatest minds that ever lived. When Newton stayed at home to avoid the 1665 plague, he discovered the laws of gravity and optics, and he invented calculus. If Isaac Newton couldn't figure out how to time the market, we should not try.

NEVER INTERRUPT COMPOUNDING UNNECESSARILY

Surprisingly, the hardest part of investing for many is getting comfortable with the inactivity required to allow your winners time to run. Selling stocks too early is a very common problem for many investors, including me, but inactivity can be the most intelligent (i.e., more rewarding) strategy if you select stocks of good businesses. There is some truth in the adage that the best investor is a dead investor.

"The first rule of compounding: Never interrupt it unnecessarily."
— CHARLIE MUNGER

If you search 'Fidelity dead investors,' you will find many consistent references. The gist of the story is that when conducting an internal review of customer performance from 2003 to 2013, Fidelity learned that the clients with the best returns were the ones who were dead and the second-best group were clients who had totally forgotten about their account: inactive accounts! It's not in Fidelity's interest to confirm the story, but it rings true. Many active investors become their own worst enemies. History shows that investors who consistently resist the urge to fiddle with their portfolio tilt the odds of success in their favor. The next time the headlines get scary, and you sense panic rising from within, remind yourself of the best-performing Fidelity accounts and then, like in a child's game, "play dead."

"In 1986, my biggest accomplishment was not doing anything stupid.
There is not much to do; there is not much available right now.
The trick is, when there is nothing to do, do nothing."
— WARREN BUFFETT

COMPOUNDING RESULTS FROM ACTUAL INVESTMENTS IN INDIVIDUAL STOCK NAMES

Now, let's shift from looking at a portfolio's compounding results to individual stock name's compounding results. These will be real-life examples from a larger collection of long-term, buy-and-hold stock names, and it will include several winners, one very big loser, and a recent addition. You will see their actual compound annual growth rates, and as promised, no new math concepts will be necessary. Importantly, the examples will also be used to introduce key elements of a buy-and-hold stock investing methodology and to highlight the benefits of investing in stocks of individual businesses instead of mutual funds.

Amazon shares were purchased on September 9, 1997, a bit more than twenty-six years ago, in a taxable investment account; the purchase was not made in the tax-deferred IRA account mentioned in the prior section. The collection has held a few stocks longer than this one (Berkshire Hathaway since 1993 and Microsoft since 1996) and some almost as long (Adobe and American Express since 1998), but none have performed, based on their compound annual growth rate, as well as Amazon for that long of a duration (26 years).

Amazon had several stock splits since the original shares were bought, and on June 6, 2022, Amazon split their shares again. This time each share became twenty shares (a twenty for one stock split). Each share split has lowered the per share cost basis, and with the June 6, 2022 split, the cost basis for purchasing Amazon stock on September 9, 1997 decreased to only seventeen cents per share. In contrast, Amazon's stock price at year-end 2023 was $152 per share.

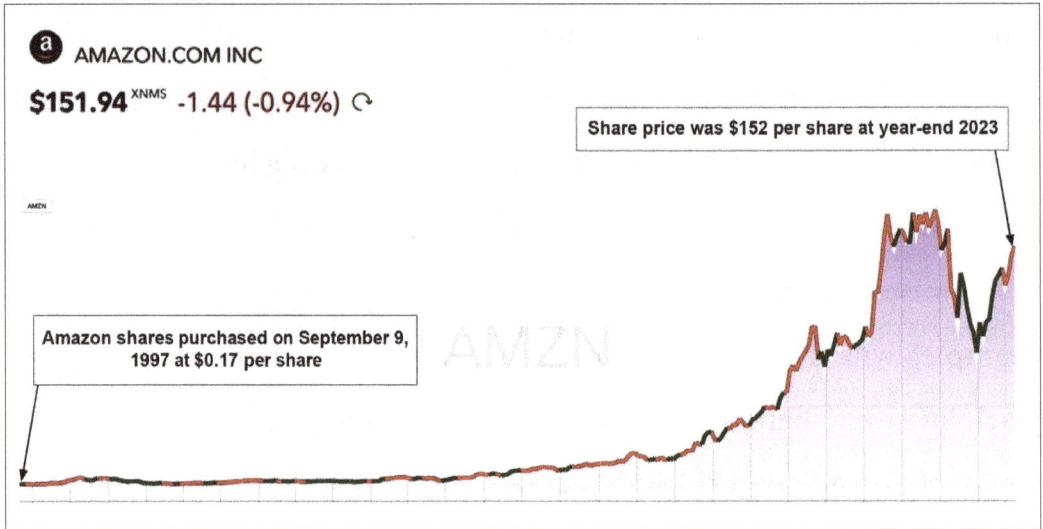

AMAZON.COM INC
$151.94 XNMS -1.44 (-0.94%)

Share price was $152 per share at year-end 2023

Amazon shares purchased on September 9, 1997 at $0.17 per share

Amazon's stock price has therefore increased to 894 times the original purchase price ($152 divided by $0.17) in about 26 years. Every $5,000 invested in 1997 would have grown to more than $4.5 million (5,000 multiplied by 894) by year-end of 2023. That is a compound annual growth rate of 30% for 26 years.

Amazon compound annual growth rate = $(152/0.17)^{(1/26)} - 1 = 30\%$ CAGR

Amazon's stock price has been volatile. It started at $170 per share in 2022 and closed that year at $84, a 51% price drop, and then the stock price rose 81% in 2023 to $152 per share. Even when the stock was down at $84 per share, the stock was still up about 500 times the purchase price, which would still equate to a 28% compound annual growth rate over 25 years. At either price, $152 or $84 per share, the unrealized profits are greater than 99% of the stock price, highlighting that investing a little now will payoff over time when you have a strong CAGR.

IT'S BETTER TO BUY A WONDERFUL BUSINESS AT A FAIR PRICE THAN A FAIR BUSINESS AT A WONDERFUL PRICE

Learning to distinguish good businesses from bad businesses is a useful skill for you to develop, if you want to create wealth by investing in stocks. This skill will be discussed more in an upcoming section, but here we will compare the investment in a fair business with that of a wonderful business, noting the differences in return.

Charlie Munger makes a comparison of a fair business and a wonderful business in a chapter, called "A Lesson on Elementary Worldly Wisdom," of the book Poor Charlie's Almanack: "Over the long term, it's hard for a stock to earn a much better return than the business which underlies it earns. If the business earns six percent on capital (annually) over forty years and you hold it for forty years, you are not going to make much more than a six percent (compound annual) return—even if you originally buy the business at a huge discount. Conversely, if a business earns eighteen percent on capital (annually) over twenty or thirty years, even if you pay an expensive looking price, you'll end up with one hell of a good result."

It can even make sense to pay a higher-than-normal price for a business that is growing rapidly and profitably if you believe it will continue for an extended period. For example, imagine you paid twice (double) the stock price to purchase the Amazon shares on September 9, 1997. You would have paid the split-adjusted price of 34 cents per share instead of 17 cents per share. Paying that higher price would have increased your risk, been wasteful and foolish, but the return after 26 years, at the end of 2023, would still be outstanding: a 26% CAGR instead of a 30% CAGR. Here is the math: $(152/0.34)^{\wedge}(1/26) - 1 = 26\%$ CAGR.

Over the long run, the impact of your purchase price is overwhelmed by rapid cashflow growth. Business quality (as measured by returns on capital and reinvestment opportunities) surpasses purchase/sale price if you hold the investment for an extended period. That is why Warren Buffett likes to say, it is better to buy a wonderful business at a fair price than a fair business at a wonderful price. And Charlie, of course, played a key role in helping Warren reach that conclusion.

"Too much of a good thing can be...wonderful."
— Mae West

In the long run (over decades), it is the quality of the business that you invested in which determines your returns. For a business to qualify as 'wonderful' quality, the scope for reinvestment opportunities makes a big difference. Growth rates tend to slow down as a company grows bigger over time, and eventually, the company only sees limited opportunities for re-investing back into the business. The potential for reinvestment opportunities is linked to the size of the market the business serves. A great business in a small niche or shrinking market has little room to grow because of the limited size of their market.

Wonderful businesses serve large and growing markets allowing them to continue growing the business for an extended period, unleashing the magic of compounding. If Amazon had decided to only sell books online, it could have dominated that market, but book sales are a relatively small market and Amazon's business would have been less wonderful than it is now. By focusing on successfully selling much more than just books, Amazon was able to expand the size of its addressable market, expanding its scope for reinvestment significantly.

If a business is truly wonderful, you can pay more for it and still do very well long-term. But if the business turns out to be less wonderful than expected or you do not hold it for an extended period, paying too much for it can impair your results.

Let's move on from Amazon and look at another good business.

Berkshire Hathaway has been a part of the collection even longer than Amazon. Berkshire has never split its shares, and since the business has consistently grown over a long period, the price per share has grown to a much larger per share amount than if it had stock splits (like Amazon did).

Berkshire hit a milestone in March 2022 when it first closed above a half million dollars per share and then it finished 2023 at $543,000 per share. The year 2023 was another milestone; it was the 30th consecutive year of Berkshire being part of the buy-and-hold portfolio. The first Berkshire share was purchased in March 1993, in a taxable investment account, at a price of $12,609.85. It is the collection's longest held stock.

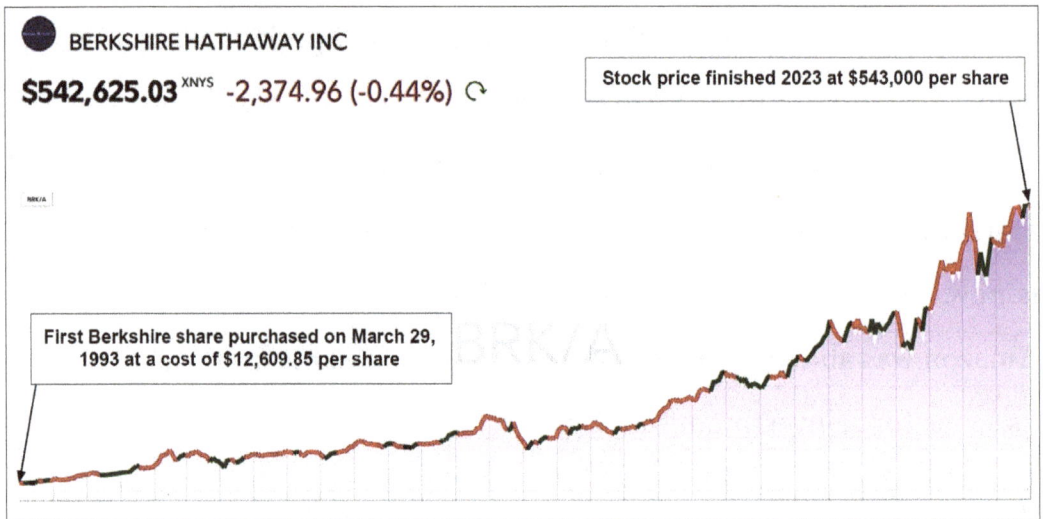

Additional shares of Berkshire Hathaway were bought at various times over the years: whenever the stock valuation was attractive and funds were available. Some Berkshire shares were sold to re-balance the portfolio in 2021, but for almost 30 years of owning Berkshire, no shares were sold. The original share that was purchased in 1993 remains in the collection today.

The stock price for the first share is 43 times higher now than its beginning value ($543,000/$12,600)], and that equates to a 13% compound annual growth rate over the last 31 years (a much lower annual compounding rate than Amazon but still better than the overall stock market). The overall annualized return for all the Berkshire shares held in the collection is a bit better than 13%, due to the timely purchase of additional shares when they were attractively priced.

$$\text{Berkshire compound annual growth rate}$$
$$= (543{,}000/12{,}600)^\wedge(1/30.75) - 1 = 13\%$$

Several other investments in the collection have generated better returns, but none have been as useful as Berkshire. You can learn about much more than investing by being associated with Berkshire Hathaway, Warren Buffett (the CEO and Chairman for the last 58 years), and Charlie Munger (the Vice Chairman, until he died very recently). Warren is 93 years old, and Charlie died on November 28, 2023 at 99 years old.

Warren has been, and Charlie was, at the pinnacle of the investing world for decades. One of Warren and Charlie's secrets to success is possessing humility and humor in abundance. Warren often said, they were a perfect partnership because Charlie can hear and Warren can see. It is not an accident that they use a lot of self-deprecatory humor. It is a key reason for their high levels of sustained success. It is required for maintaining sanity and will enable you to have a long, wonderful ride.

Although Berkshire has been a great investment for more than 30 years, it would have been much, much better if you had invested that same amount in Berkshire stock 50 years ago, instead of 30 years ago. Remember, the eighth wonder of the world: compounding. Berkshire's stock price per share in 1973 was only $71 per share, so $12,600 would have bought 177.5 shares in 1973; today those shares would be worth $96 million $(177.5{*}543,000)$.

The outcome of $96 million is a 20% compound annual growth rate over 50 years (compared to the 13% CAGR for the 30-year investment). This example shows how having extra time for compounding to occur plus a higher growth rate can make an incredible difference. Amazing, but accurate!

Berkshire CAGR from 1973 to 2023 = $(543,000/71)^{\wedge}(1/50) - 1 = 19.58\% = 20\%$

Even if you had bought only a $1,000 worth of Berkshire Hathaway shares in 1973, it would have grown to a value of almost $8 million at the end of 2023, and all you would have had to do after purchasing the stock was hold the shares and watch it grow. Even when the $1,000 is adjusted for inflation, it only becomes $4,000 in today's dollars ($1,000 multiplied by 1.03 fifty times). Money can be very tight, but a cheaper car, a less expensive apartment, and so on could allow many young people to save $4,000 quickly, and it could become millions if you invest it for long enough. Invest as much as you can as early as you can. Deferred delights are only deferred; they will come soon enough, and your future self will be proud of your current self.

"It's waiting that helps you as an investor and a lot of people just can't stand to wait. If you didn't get the deferred -gratification gene, you've got to work very hard to overcome that."
— CHARLIE MUNGER

A third, more recently purchased business in the collection of buy-and-hold investments is Tesla. The first Tesla shares were purchased about eight years ago, also in a taxable account. Tesla's stock price has been volatile (but the business is fascinating) and the financial results have been worth the stress. I have not seen a company as large and complex execute as well as Tesla has; I do not say that lightly. Tesla's business performance has been off the charts. Their earnings have been growing rapidly and are likely, but not guaranteed, to be materially higher ten and twenty years from now.

The original Tesla shares were bought in December 2015 and early in 2016 at an average cost of $15.58 per share. The stock price was relatively flat for the first four years but then rose rapidly. The stock price reached highs above $400 per share late in 2021 but fell 70% to $108 per share at the start of 2023. Tesla's stock price rose 130% in 2023, ending the year at a stock price of $248 per share. The year-end stock price is up 16 times in the 8 years since purchased with a compound annual growth rate of 41% (a higher compound annual return than Amazon but over a much shorter period with holding periods of 8 years for Tesla versus 26 years for Amazon).

TESLA INC

$248.48 XNMS -4.70 (-1.86%)

Stock price was $248 per share at year-end 2023

Stock price reached highs above $400 per share late in 2021

Tesla shares purchased from December 2015 through early in 2016 at an average cost of $15.58 per share

Tesla compound annual growth rate = $(248/15.58)^{(1/8)} - 1 = 41\%$

LONG-TERM, BUY-AND-HOLD COLLECTION

The three stocks covered thus far (Amazon, Berkshire, and Tesla) and the three briefly mentioned (Microsoft, Adobe and American Express) are only part of the collection of good businesses. The total number of stock names in the buy-and-hold collection averages to about ten at any specific point over the last twenty years. There have been additions to, and a few removals from, the collection but only gradually. For example, one company, Kinder Morgan, was taken private so it had to be sold. AOL and Cisco were sold at irresistibly high stock valuations relative to the intrinsic value of the underlying business, and a few others have been removed or added because business conditions changed. The buy-and-hold collection at every point in time has been a very diverse group of businesses. Just looking at the ones mentioned thus far provides a sense for how diverse it is. The investment accounts have also been used to invest in oil production companies at various times but using a different strategy; those stock names are not included in the buy-and-hold collection.

Time is the friend of good businesses since their stock price should eventually rise if you hold the shares for long enough. There may be unpleasant surprises like discovering you paid too much initially, but a good business's intrinsic value should continue to grow. In the long run, its stock will likely win. A diverse portfolio of stocks in good businesses is only risky when your holding period isn't long enough. The easiest way to increase your odds of success is to increase your holding period.

"Rule No. 1: Never Lose Money.

Rule No. 2: Never Forget Rule No. 1"

— Warren Buffett

The two rules in Warren's quote above may sound basic, but they are deeper than many realize. Warren clearly wants to make money, but Warren, Charlie, and many of the most successful investors first focus on not losing money. Frequent losses can turn even extraordinary results into poor overall results. The inverse is also true: avoiding losses can allow very normal outcomes to outperform overall. Warren has said, "I don't try to jump over 7-foot hurdles; I look for 1-foot hurdles I can step over." Warren can get away with more normal outcomes, and still win overall against other investors because he avoids losses.

Many people want to get rich quickly. Getting rich quicker than what you can reasonably expect from a buy-and-hold stock investing strategy would often require you to invest in ways that are equivalent to being able to jump over 7-foot hurdles. Trying that will result in more losses than stepping over 1-foot hurdles. Each successful 7-foot hurdle will be very impressive, but when combined with the more frequent losses, your overall result will be underperformance.

The buy-and-hold collection has only had one long-held stock with a negative return. It started with an emotional purchase, a mistake. I paid a high-share price, even knowing that it was a high price, because I had a fear of missing out (FOMO) on a very popular stock. The experience worsened when, several years later, an unexpected new competitor arrived, crushed everyone else, and grabbed almost all of the market sector's profits.

The FOMO stock was Nokia. Nokia was purchased at $46.77 per share on April 4, 2000. At year-end 2023, the stock price was $3.42 per share, a -93% unrealized loss. The new competitor was Apple when it released the iPhone in 2007. Nokia is no longer considered to be a part of the long-term, buy-and-hold collection. It would be a dirty lump of coal amongst the other sparkling jewels.

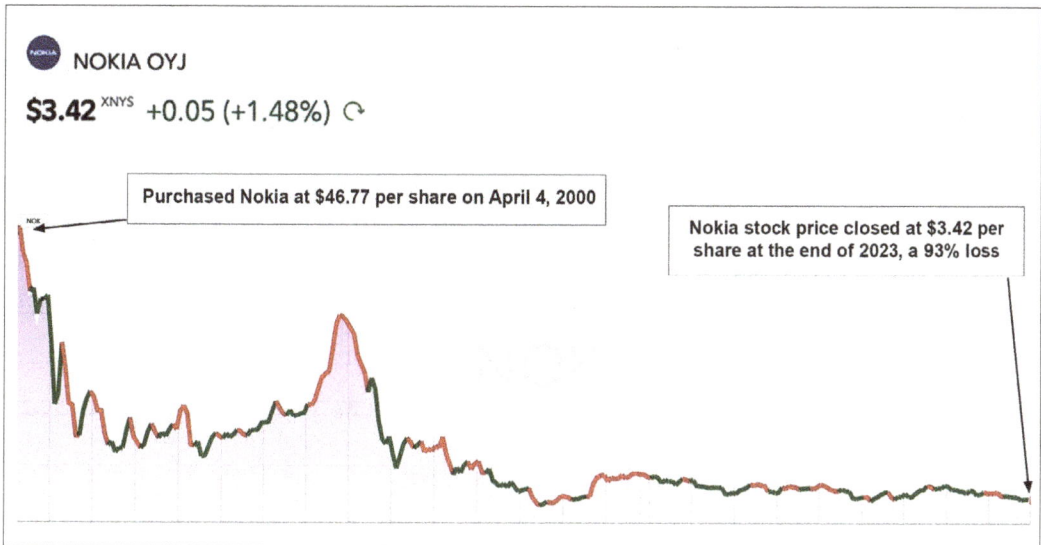

NOKIA OYJ

$3.42 XNYS +0.05 (+1.48%) ↻

Purchased Nokia at $46.77 per share on April 4, 2000

Nokia stock price closed at $3.42 per share at the end of 2023, a 93% loss

The real hit from Nokia is not the value loss. The hit that stings the most is I could have invested that money in a stock that had much better returns. For example, the total Nokia investment was $37,415.35. The same amount invested into Amazon shares on April 4, 2000, would be worth more than $2 million today. (Amazon's share price was only $2.76 per share on April 4, 2000 and $152 per share at year-end 2023.) The growth that was lost, after 23 years of compounding, is many times the value of the initial investment in Nokia.

You may be thinking to yourself that selecting Amazon to compare as the alternative is being too harsh. Regrettably, it is not. I sold some Amazon shares, thankfully not all, in December 1999, just a few months prior to investing in Nokia. I relished my Amazon holdings and was delighted with how the business was executing at the time. However, the stock had risen rapidly, and the stock valuation appeared to be high. Amazon had become a very large portion of my portfolio, so some of the shares in the collection were sold to re-balance, like the business schools preach. The value loss from the Nokia purchase is about $35,000. That is obviously not good, but the real hit to wealth was missing out on millions of dollars of Amazon stock price upside.

It still stings to think about Nokia, more than 23 years later. I continue to hold the stock as a lesson reminder. Seeing the Nokia loss in the account rubs my nose in the emotional purchase mistake. It also serves as a reminder to pause before heeding someone else's advice to sell even a portion of a winner. Furthermore, the Nokia shares are in a tax-deferred account, the spouse's IRA, so there would be no tax benefits if the Nokia shares were sold.

Thankfully, there is a positive lesson from the Nokia experience; it illustrates another major benefit of buy-and-hold investing. You can be wrong. You can even be very wrong like the Nokia purchase, but when you are a long-term, buy-and-hold investor of individual stock names one mega-winner like Amazon, Berkshire, Tesla, and others can more than cover the losses from your losers. That is how stock investing can work for you. Your winners can much more than pay for your losers. Your winners can be up multiple times their beginning value, if you hold them long enough, but your losers can only lose their full beginning value. A loser's absolute worst-case scenario is having a value of zero.

A DIVERSIFIED COLLECTION OF STOCKS IN GOOD BUSINESSES SHOULD WIN IF THE STOCKS ARE HELD LONG ENOUGH

The major insight for you to take away from the Nokia experience is, if you hold a diversified collection of stocks in good businesses, you really should not lose money overall if the stocks are held long enough (held for decades). Long-term, buy-and-hold winners with ending values that are up ten, twenty, forty, or more times their beginning values should more than pay for the number of losers you own.

I will not review all of the long-held stock experiences to avoid repetition, but with the exception of Nokia, each stock has been a compounding machine, creating wealth that is much more than the amount of savings invested. Each is also now a large business, but it is important to note that they were much smaller when the original shares were purchased.

LAW OF LARGE NUMBERS

The purchase of a smaller-sized business at the beginning matters because, as mentioned previously, the growth rate (CAGR) becomes increasingly difficult to maintain as a business expands. This is informally referred to in business as the "Law of Large Numbers." This effect is why you will often see growth rates decline as companies grow bigger over time. For example, for Tesla to grow electric vehicle deliveries at a 50% CAGR ten years ago, it only had to have an annual increase of 10,000 vehicles (when the beginning value was 20,000 vehicles). However, in 2024, a 50% CAGR requires a 1 million annual delivery increase when sales are running at a 2 million per year rate. As another example, Amazon's percentage growth rate outlook was much higher in 1997 than it is now. The stock market valued Amazon at only $1.5 billion in 1997, but it is now 1,000 times larger with a year-end 2023 stock price valuation of $1.6 trillion. A high growth rate may last for a while, but at some point, even with the best businesses, growth rates will start to slow because of the law of large numbers.

OWN SEVERAL STOCK NAMES FOR DECADES BY THE TIME YOU REACH RETIREMENT AGE

I began to invest rationally in 1990 when the IRA account was opened. I decided then that I wanted to have owned several stocks of good businesses for decades by the time I reached retirement age. It was an experiment to test the buy-and-hold methodology as well as a goal. The goal is quite modest in some ways since it requires that you do less, not more, which is much less trading activity than the average investor. The experiment has been useful and lucrative yet very few people hold a stock name continuously for decades. Ask around. Some people will talk favorably about buy-and-hold investing, but you will likely find out they have not actually held any stock name for decades, except for their employer's stock in a few cases. If your experience mimics mine, most people will rattle off a list of stock names they wish they had not sold.

"Calling someone who trades actively in the market
an investor is like calling someone who repeatedly engages
in one-night stands a romantic."
— WARREN BUFFETT

If you decide to set a similar buy-and-hold goal, and I suggest you do, you should include some smaller companies that have the potential to become long-term compounding machines. A counterargument is that bigger businesses can have some material advantages over smaller businesses, and I would agree. I am not arguing against investing in big businesses, and I will continue to hold big businesses in my collection. I am only suggesting that you also search for smaller businesses to add to your collection as well. Smaller businesses may have a longer runway for growth, will add diversity to your collection, and may not stay small for long if your decision to purchase proves to be a good one.

As an example, NU Holdings, a smaller business, was recently added to the buy-and-hold collection. I decided to add NU shares in June 2023, so it is a very new addition. NU is growing rapidly and became profitable only recently, less than two years ago. NU is a high-quality, disruptive business that provides a smartphone-based digital banking platform and digital financial services in Brazil, Mexico, and Colombia. The challenge is no matter how wonderful the business appears to be, the future will be uncertain so you should also pay an attractive (low) price; however, good businesses often have high stock market valuations for extended periods of time.

NU's stock price had risen rapidly right before I decided to purchase shares, so I used a different approach to acquire the stock. Instead of buying stock directly, NU stock options were sold starting in June 2023 in a tax-deferred account. Stock options and the selling options strategy will be covered in detail in an upcoming section but using options to build a position in NU was more lucrative than if I had bought the stock directly. NU's stock price was $8.33 per share at year-end 2023. When you credit the gains from selling NU options, the outcome resulted in purchasing 73,800 NU shares at an effective cost that was 27% below the stock price at year-end. The plan is to both continue to hold shares for capital appreciation as well as to continue to sell options with NU.

BUY-AND-HOLD TAX BENEFITS

Many of the buy-and-hold collection's best performing stocks were bought in taxable accounts: Berkshire Hathaway, Microsoft, Amazon, Tesla, and more. Beyond the power of compounding, each one also showed the tax benefits that come along with buying and holding stocks of "winning" companies over long periods of time.

By holding stocks for long periods and not selling, you not only benefit when a stock's value continues to increase over time, but when held in taxable accounts, you also reap tax benefits by deferring tax payments on the unrealized gains. The tax benefits of a buy-and-hold approach are a very simple effect. Charlie Munger discussed it, but you have probably never heard it discussed by investment helpers. If you are going to buy something which compounds for thirty years at 15% per annum and you pay one 35% tax at the very end, the way that works out is that after taxes, you keep 13.3% per annum. In contrast, if you bought the same investment but had to pay taxes every year of 35% of the 15% that you earned, then your return would be 15% minus 35% of 15% or only 9.75% per year compounded. So, the difference between the after-tax returns, 13.3% minus 9.75%, is over 3.5%. And what a 3.5% annual compounding difference does to numbers over long holding periods like 30 years is truly eye-opening.

Let's quantify the buy-and-hold tax benefits here (refer to the 30-year 'Eye-Opening' graph below). Assume thirty years ago you invested $25,000 in a taxable account, and the investments grew at a 15% CAGR before tax:

- A buy and hold methodology would have an after-tax CAGR of 13.3% and an ending value of $1,058,857, growing 42 times larger than the beginning value after-tax.

- An active investor (trader) or a mutual fund with a high turnover rate that sold stocks and bought new ones each year would have an after-tax CAGR of 9.75% and an ending value of $407,451, growing only 16 times larger than the beginning value.

- The after-tax wealth difference is huge and in favor of a buy-and-hold strategy with individual stock names. Even when the investments grow at the same compound annual growth rate before tax, the buy-and-hold strategy with individual stock names after thirty years results in more than double the wealth after taxes are taken into account.

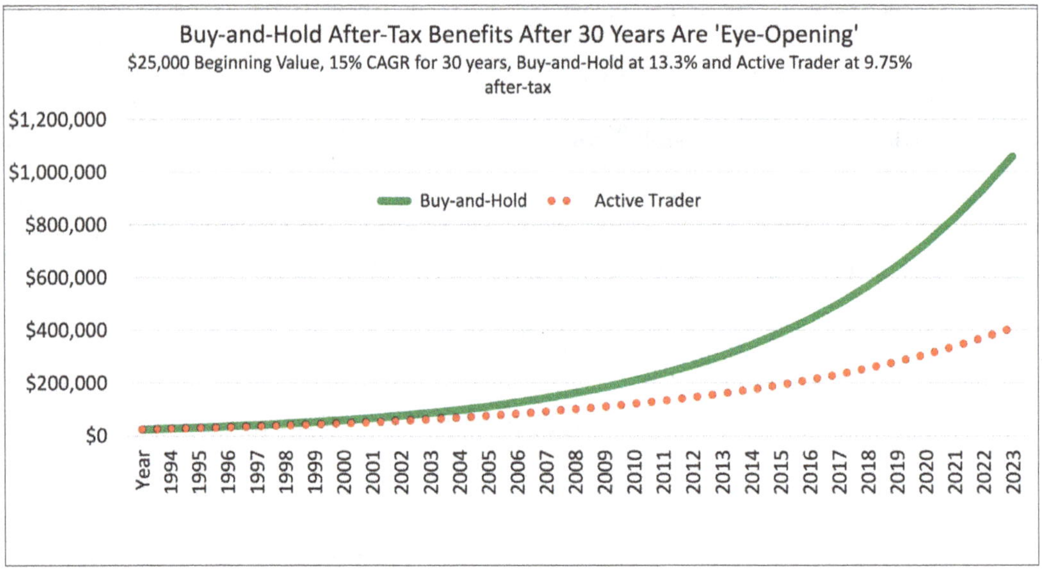

Importantly, the after-tax wealth difference will continue to grow when you expand beyond 30 years. After 40 years, if you invest in something which compounds at 15% per annum and you pay one 35% tax at the very end, you keep 13.77% per annum after-tax, an improved after-tax growth rate versus the 13.3% per annum after 30 years. The same beginning value of $25,000 used in the example above now becomes $4.4 million after-tax after 40 years. In contrast, if an active investor (trader) earned the same 15% CAGR before-tax for 40 years, the active investor would only have $1.0 million after tax.

The buy-and-hold strategy (in individual stock names) outperforms again, and this time it does it by creating more than four times the wealth because of the longer holding period and the slightly higher after-tax compounding rate. Refer to the 40-year 'Jaw-Dropping' graph below. The potential to have four-times more wealth when you buy-and-hold individual stock names versus actively trade, or invest in an actively traded mutual fund, is a huge difference yet most investors are unaware of it. Many financial helpers are probably also unaware, and even those that may know are unlikely to mention it to you because they are much more highly incentivized to sell you mutual fund investments.

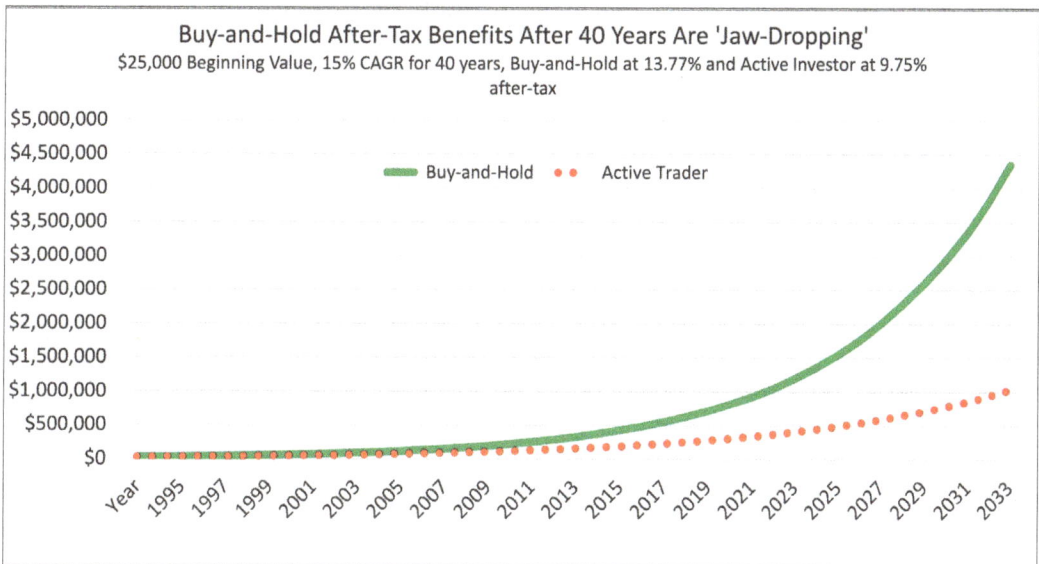

Buy-and-Hold After-Tax Benefits After 40 Years Are 'Jaw-Dropping'
$25,000 Beginning Value, 15% CAGR for 40 years, Buy-and-Hold at 13.77% and Active Investor at 9.75% after-tax

If you invest in great companies in a taxable account, hold the shares for long stretches of time, sit back, and do nothing. You can get a huge edge just from the way income taxes work. With mutual funds in contrast, even if you never sell any of your shares in the mutual fund, you will still have to pay taxes annually on your share of any capital gains incurred by the fund. Some funds, especially actively managed funds, turn over their holdings frequently. Your share of the distributed capital gains will add up, impairing your result, and the impairments will become large after an extended time period. The mutual fund's historical returns, as published in their prospectus, will not include the tax impairments.

COMPOUND ANNUAL GROWTH RATE TARGETS

My strong preference is to invest in individual stock names instead of mutual funds. Investing in individual stock names, being a collector of good businesses, has been much more lucrative, fun, and interesting than investing in mutual funds. I target a 15% compound annual growth rate over the long-term for my overall portfolio of buy-and-hold stock investments. I have a higher target when selling options: 20% compound annual growth rate target for the selling options portfolio. Actual results overall have exceeded each target thus far.

However, most people invest in mutual funds. The best outcome that you can reasonably expect by investing in mutual funds is 7-9% CAGR, if the long-term average of a 10% CAGR for the US stock market can be maintained, not guaranteed, in the future. The average stock market investor's returns are even worse and less than a 6% CAGR.

Warren is often asked, "Warren, your investing approach (a long-term, buy-and-hold stock investing strategy) is so simple, why doesn't everyone copy you?" You may be asking the same question—and if you are, it is a great question. Warren has sometimes answered that question with the reply, "Because nobody wants to get rich slow." Buy good businesses, don't overpay, and hold them as long as they remain good businesses; it just seems too easy. Successfully investing in the stock market is not a get-rich-quick-scheme, but another prevalent reason that more people do not copy Warren Buffett's investing approach is because very few people encourage it. Multitudes of people, an entire industry (financial services), actively discourage it.

MUTUAL FUNDS

Investment advisers and stockbrokers will make a lot more money from fees and commissions, with much less effort, if you invest in mutual funds instead of buying and holding individual stocks. Investors (you) may not see the mutual fund fees directly. Many are hidden as "transactional costs" and not included in the "expense ratio" listed on the prospectus. Mutual funds pay brokers directly for adding investors to their mutual funds. Essentially, the mutual funds are bribing brokers to betray their client (you) and put the client's money into a high-commission product; it's sad, but accurate, and this has worked to produce a huge amount of mutual fund sales.

The average stock investor will do worse than the stock market's overall average growth rate because of fees and ineffective behaviors. Both are common in the world of stock investing; as just one of many examples, many people that try to time the market will instead discover that they bought in at a high price point or sold at a relatively low point and will not enjoy average returns. Those unforced errors add up, and when combined with fees, the average investor likely earns a compound annual growth rate well below 6%—a rate well below the stock market's 10% rule of thumb and even further below the buy-and-hold collection's 15% CAGR target. Compounding annually at a 6% rate versus a 15% rate is a huge difference. Recall that even small differences in compound annual growth rates over long periods will create vastly different results (wealth).

To be clear, even if you do not want to invest in individual stocks, you should still invest money in the stock market because growth rates are better in the stock market than in most alternatives (real estate, bonds, gold, and so on). Actively managed mutual funds overall have a terrible track record; the primary reason is expenses. So, if you decide to invest in mutual funds, stick with low-cost index funds; index funds are sometimes called passive funds versus the alternative of actively managed funds.

"When trillions of dollars are managed by Wall Streeters charging high fees, it will usually be the managers who reap outsized profits, not the clients (you). Both large and small investors (you) should stick with low-cost index funds."

— Warren Buffett

Your best approach with mutual funds is to 'dollar-cost-average' your savings into low-cost stock market index funds. Dollar-cost-averaging involves investing the same amount of money in the fund at regular intervals over a certain period of time, regardless of the index fund's share price. By using dollar-cost averaging, over time you may lower your average cost per share and reduce the impact of market volatility on your account. If you contribute savings regularly into a very low-cost index fund, you will likely do better than the average investor but will still be a bit below the overall stock market's average CAGR.

Most people should probably invest exclusively in low-cost index funds especially when you are just starting to invest and are early in the learning curve. If you are less than twenty-five years old and a good saver, passive investing exclusively in low-cost index funds may turn out fine because a 7 to 9% compound annual growth rate over a long period (if you start young) will probably still result in acceptable levels of wealth. If you have less time to build wealth, you will probably need to save much more money and/or earn higher growth rates than what you can reasonably expect to earn from mutual funds.

You should tread carefully whenever you are passing through financial services' territory and that includes the mutual fund industry, but there is one name that is unique and worth mentioning: the Vanguard Group. John Bogle founded the Vanguard Group in 1974. John Bogle revolutionized the mutual fund world by creating index investing, which allows investors to buy mutual funds that track the broader market. He did this with the overall intent to make investing easier and at a low cost for the average investor.

John Bogle then did something very beneficial for investors when he gave company ownership to the shareholders of the Vanguard mutual funds: investor ownership. In short, Vanguard is a company owned by the investor and for the investor. When you own shares in a Vanguard mutual fund, you are an owner of the company that offers it. Vanguard's investor ownership structure removes the incentive to charge high fees.

Sadly, no other mutual fund company followed Bogle's example. When you buy shares in any other non-Vanguard mutual fund, you are not the owner, and their owners (shareholders or private owners) are incentivized to charge excessive fees and have hidden expenses.

The unique ownership structure is the reason Vanguard generally has the lowest cost mutual funds in the industry. In addition, Vanguard's presence in the industry puts competitive pressure that probably restrains the others from being even more expensive than they are.

Your independent mind may have decided to enter the room, asking, "Why would Bogle do that?" Thinking independently is a wonderful thing, and that is another great question. John Bogle would have been much, much wealthier had he retained ownership of Vanguard instead of giving it away to the fund shareholders like he did. The answer is John was a good man, one of humanity's finest.

"If a statue is ever erected to honor the person who has done the most

for American investors, the hands down choice should be Jack [John]

Bogle. For decades, Jack has urged investors to invest in ultra-low-cost

index funds. In his crusade, he amassed only a tiny percentage of the

wealth that has typically flowed to managers who have promised their

investors large rewards while delivering them nothing – or, as in our

bet, less than nothing – of added value. In his early years, Jack was

frequently mocked by the investment-management industry. Today,

however, he has the satisfaction of knowing that he helped millions

of investors realize far better returns on their savings than they

otherwise would have earned. He is a hero to them and to me."

— WARREN BUFFETT

When my buy-and-hold experiment started in the early 1990s, I also started a parallel experiment with mutual funds. Money was added consistently for several years into seven different mutual funds during the 1990s, two were Vanguard funds. As I became more experienced and comfortable investing in individual stock names (and because the mutual funds, after careful monitoring, were underperforming), I started to wind down the mutual funds, except for two in specialized sectors that I continue to own today.

One of the still open mutual fund accounts is Vanguard Health Care, opened in September 1993. The records are incomplete prior to 2003, but the Health Care fund has averaged an 11% CAGR before taxes since 2003, for the last 21 years. The other open mutual fund is Columbia's Acorn, an actively managed fund that specialized in small and mid-sized businesses. The Acorn account was opened in July 1994. The records for Acorn are also incomplete prior to 2003. The investment value in the Acorn fund has averaged a 9% CAGR before taxes for the last 21 years.

Even though money was never withdrawn from, or added to, the two open funds during the last 21 years, fund holders pay taxes annually on their share of any capital gains incurred by the fund. Taxes were paid on those gains with money from a separate account so the 11% and 9% CAGRs are over-stated and would be lower for both funds if the ending values were reduced by the cumulative taxes paid during the 21-year period. However, the records are not complete enough to determine how much lower.

Your inner voice, or voices, may be saying something like this:

"Okay...We have a dilemma. Looks like we will need to decide which way we should go: Invest in stocks of publicly traded businesses or invest in mutual funds? Becoming a buy-and-hold collector of good businesses could be more lucrative than investing in mutual funds. The differences in wealth over the long-term could be huge...but no one else seems to be doing that. Going against the crowd can be scary. It may fail. we could look like an idiot if it fails. Mutual funds look to be the more conventional approach, and it sounds less risky...but conventional sounds average and the average person is almost broke...Hasn't Buffett made fun of the fact that too many people behave as lemmings?"

"(For most)...Failing conventionally is the route to go; as a group, lemmings may have a rotten image, but no individual lemming has ever received bad press."
— WARREN BUFFET

You do not have to make a choice between two paths. You have a third choice. You could do both. I did. To be clear, I have tilted almost completely towards investing in individual stocks over time, but I started by doing both initially: investing in the stocks of good businesses as well as investing in mutual funds. You will need to decide for yourself. The main thing is that you start; don't dither, plus I strongly suggest you avoid investing in actively managed funds and just stick to low-cost, index funds (like Vanguard) for your mutual fund investments.

The hope from sharing real-world compounding experiences is to encourage young people to harness the power of time and start to invest early, as early as you can. Even small amounts of savings can snowball into massive amounts over time. Let's now discuss how you can get started.

DEVELOP A HABIT OF SAVING AND BEGIN COMPOUNDING EARLY

Spending less than you make is fundamental to saving enough money to start investing as early as possible. Most behavior is habitual, and you can develop a habit of saving. Samuel Johnson, in the eighteenth century, guides you on how to create a habit. He observed "the chains of habit are too weak to be felt until they are too strong to be broken."

A simple way to learn the habit of saving is to make it automatic. This is probably advice you have heard before, but that does not make it any less effective. Set up automatic transfers directly from your paycheck, as soon as you get paid, into your investment accounts (401-K, tax-advantaged retirement, taxable investment, and any mutual fund accounts). That way you are never touching the money yourself; it is just going right into your investment accounts at regular intervals. Then, each time you get a pay raise increase the amount you transfer, if you can, to up to about 20% of your base salary; perhaps, you could do more, but you should also enjoy life and be generous and charitable.

> *"Do not save what is left after spending*
> *but spend what is left after saving."*
> —WARREN BUFFETT

You will need to have an additional amount of money in a bank checking account to use for day-to-day spending and to maintain a savings or money-market account for use as a large emergency fund. Your daily spending and emergency funds should be separate from investment funds. With that separation, the retirement and investment accounts can be fully invested in long-term stock market investments. No one gets wealthy from a savings account, so after your emergency fund is fully funded, put your money to work creating wealth by investing in stocks.

Your first $100,000 will be the most difficult, then it gets easier		
Net Worth Change	Years to Achieve	% of Total Time
$27K - $100K	9.37	32%
$100K - $200K	4.96	17%
$200K - $300K	2.90	10%
$300K- $400K	2.06	7%
$400K - $500K	1.60	5%
$500K - $600K	1.30	4%
$600K - $700K	1.10	4%
$700K - $800K	0.96	3%
$800K - $900K	0.84	3%
$900K - $1M	0.75	3%
$1M - $1.1M	0.68	2%
$1.1M - $1.2M	0.62	2%
$1.2M - $1.3M	0.57	2%
$1.3M - $1.4M	0.53	2%
$1.4M - $1.5M	0.49	2%
$1.5M - $1.6M	0.46	2%
Total Time:	29.21	100%
Assumes $27,000 grows at 15% CAGR		

You should also track the value of your investments and your net worth growth annually. Create a simple spreadsheet that can be updated at least annually. The spreadsheet sums up how much you have—in checking, emergency fund, 401-K, tax-advantaged retirement, taxable investment accounts, and mutual funds—and then subtracts any amounts you owe.

Do not get discouraged if it takes longer than you expected to reach your first $100,000 of stock investments. The first $100,000 will be the most difficult. The amount you save will be more important than your investment returns when you are below $100,000. After you pass that $100,000 threshold, you can ease your foot off the saving's pedal a bit. The road gets easier as compounding effects become more noticeable, and the subsequent $100,000 milestones will occur faster and faster all thanks to the effects of compounding!

WRAP UP: MAGIC OF COMPOUNDING AND BUY-AND-HOLD METHODOLOGY

A summary and suggestions:

- Compounding results over the long-term (decades) are simply not naturally intuitive. If they were, young people would be much more motivated to save and start investing earlier.

- Compounding results can appear slow at first, when the values are small, but the amounts really ramp up in the later periods with startling effects.

- You need to know how to calculate Compound Annual Growth Rate (CAGR) to truly understand compounding.

- The longer you wait to start saving and investing, the more you will have to save to reach a wealth goal later. Start early, start now.
  - In the actual example shown, only $27,000 had to be saved to reach

Wealthy & Wise

$1.6 million in 29 years. Contributions from savings are less than 2% of the $1.6 million.

- ○ No one wishes they started investing later in life. They wish they started earlier.

- The number of years matters: compounding goes slow until it goes fast. $27,000 of savings growing at a 15% CAGR is:
  - ○ only $100,000 after 10 years,
  - ○ becomes $400,000 after 20 years,
  - ○ is $1.8 million after 30 years,
  - ○ and $7.2 million after 40 years,
  - ○ and $29.3 million after 50 years.

- Growth rates matter: Even small differences in CAGRs over decades will create vastly different levels of wealth.

- Therefore, it is useful to learn, as early as you can, how to increase the compound annual growth rates that you can achieve with your investments.

- Use CAGR to compare two or more alternative investments. Historical, long-term average CAGRs vary significantly:
  - ○ Historical inflation at 3%,
  - ○ Bonds and US Treasuries at 4-5%,
  - ○ Average stock investor at less than 6%,
  - ○ Savings deposited consistently into a very low-cost index fund, 7-9%

Page 61

- ○ Overall US stock market at 10%,

- ○ Actual investing results from a long-term, buy-and-hold methodology with stocks of good businesses in an actual IRA account over 29 years, 15%,

- ○ Target shown for a collection of long-term, buy-and-hold investments in good businesses at 15%,

- ○ Actual investments held in some individual stocks for more than 20 years were as high as 30%.

- You must invest if you want to create real wealth. Cash, or savings that earn an interest rate that is less than the inflation rate, will steadily erode in value when adjusted for inflation.

- Modest savings invested early enough in a collection of good businesses will become compounding machines that over time create levels of wealth well beyond what you saved and invested.

- Investing outcomes of a long-term, buy-and-hold methodology—with stocks of good businesses—can beat the average CAGR for the US stock market.

- ○ Successful investing is not about timing the market. It is about time in the market.

- ○ If the businesses continue to perform well, you should ignore the stock price and just hold onto your shares.

- ○ To repeat, do not try to time the market. No one has ever done so reliably. Hold your collection through bull and bear markets.

If Isaac Newton couldn't figure out how to time the market, you should not try.

o A key rationale for buy-and-hold investing is that you will make far more money by holding through bull markets (booms) than you lose by holding through bear markets (crashes) and that was consistent with the actual experiences shown.

o Do not interrupt compounding unnecessarily. Learn to be comfortable with the inactivity required. The next time the headlines get scary, and you sense panic rising from within, remind yourself of the best-performing Fidelity accounts and then, like in a child's game, "play dead."

o Better to buy a wonderful business at a fair price than a fair business at a wonderful price. It can even make sense to pay a higher-than-normal purchase price for a business that is growing rapidly and profitably if you believe it will continue for an extended period.

o In the long run (over decades), it is the quality of the business that you invested in which determines your returns.

o Learn to distinguish good businesses from bad. How to make that distinction is covered in an upcoming section of this book.

o Invest as much as you can as early as you can. Deferred delights are only deferred. They will come soon enough, and your future self will be proud of your current self.

o Time is a good business's friend since the intrinsic business value will continue to grow and the stock price should eventually rise if you hold them long enough.

o   Set a goal to have owned several stock names in good businesses for decades by the time you reach retirement age.

o   A diversified collection of stocks in good businesses, should win (not lose money overall) if the stocks are held long enough. Long-term, buy-and-hold winners can more than pay for the number of losers you can reasonably expect.

o   Own a diverse collection of good businesses.

o   No matter how wonderful the business is, you will also want to buy it at an attractive (low) price.

o   Remember the "law of large numbers": as a business expands, at some point, even with the best businesses, growth rates will start to slow.

o   Seek to have some smaller businesses in your collection. Smaller businesses may have a longer runway for growth, can add diversity to your collection, and may not stay small for long if your decision to purchase proves to be a good one.

o   By holding stocks for long periods of time and not selling, you not only benefit when a stock's value continues to increase over time but also reap large tax benefits by deferring tax payments on the unrealized gains. If you invest in great companies, hold the shares for long stretches, sit back, and do nothing. You can get a huge edge just from the way that income taxes work (Figure 5 and 6).

- The author's strong preference is to invest in individual stock names, instead of mutual funds, since it has been much more lucrative, interesting, and fun.

- If you buy stocks in good businesses, don't overpay, and hold them (for decades) you will become a collector using a long-term, buy-and-hold methodology; this approach will have substantial advantages compared to mutual fund investments and more active stock investing strategies. The wealth difference after decades is huge and in favor of the buy-and-hold strategy.

- Two reasons more people do not copy a long-term, buy-and-hold stock investing strategy is because very few people encourage it and multitudes of people, an entire industry (financial services), actively discourage it.

- Even if you do not want to invest in individual stock names, you should still invest in the stock market, because growth rates are better in the stock market than most alternatives.

- Avoid actively managed mutual funds.

- Stick to low-cost, index funds, if you invest in mutual funds, and expect returns (7-9% historically) that are better than an average investor but below the market's overall average.

- Most people should probably invest exclusively in low-cost, index funds, especially when you are just starting to invest and early in the learning curve.

- If you have less time to build wealth, you will probably need to save much more and/or earn higher growth rates than what you can reasonably expect to earn from mutual funds.

- Spending less than you make will be key to saving enough money to start investing and compounding as early as possible. Start now.

- Your daily spending and emergency funds should be separate from investment funds. With that separation, the retirement and investment accounts can be fully invested in long-term stock market investments.

- Track the value of your investments and your growth in net worth annually.

- Do not get discouraged if reaching your first $100,000 of stock investments takes longer than you expect. The first $100,000 will be the most difficult, but it gets easier after that.

WE THINK LESS THAN
WE THINK WE THINK

Emotions intensify when dealing with money. Successful investors learn how to be rational and keep their emotions in check when they make investment decisions. Therefore, before we discuss how to select stocks of good businesses for long-term investments, let's discuss how humans think.

"Simple it's not, I'm afraid you will find,
for a mind maker-upper to make up his mind."
— DR. SEUSS

The power of investing goes beyond the ability to make you wealthy. Investing also develops your ability to think independently; it provides incentives and countless opportunities to develop and enhance your mental capabilities in reasoning, imagination, and empathy—traits crucial to your overall wellbeing. Successful investors become learning machines. As Eleanor Roosevelt observed, "Great minds discuss ideas; average minds discuss events; small minds discuss people." Once you attain a level of financial independence, your primary goal for investing should be to stay engaged in ideas and build awareness of what is happening in the world.

"Ideas shape the course of history."

— John Maynard Keynes

There is a reason I wrote the original edition of Wealthy & Wise instead of simply discussing the material verbally with family and friends. Investing is unfamiliar territory for many, and people seldom listen fully to the people talking to them. Instead, you listen to your own internal dialogue, the unspoken conversations you have with yourself. In fact, the conversation you listen to most often is not the person speaking but instead the little voice in your own head.

"There is a difference between truly listening and
waiting for your turn to talk."

— Ralph Waldo Emerson

Someone can be proposing something to you verbally and instead of listening to what they are saying you may be listening to your own running monologue of thoughts. Things like, "Why do that at all?" "I'm getting hungry. I wonder if we will have lunch?" "Hope this wraps up soon. I have lots to do today." "Why would I do that now?" and so on.

The life hack I am offering you is this: if you want to know someone has listened to your ideas, have them first read your ideas in writing, instead of only discussing it. Writing puts your voice in the reader's head. They will listen to your ideas when they read them, and importantly, you are more likely to be effective in changing their behavior by writing than you would be by just speaking to them about your ideas.

"A book is made from a tree. It is an assemblage of flat, flexible parts (still called "leaves") imprinted with dark pigmented squiggles. One glance at it and you hear the voice of another person, perhaps someone dead for thousands of years. Across the millennia, the author is speaking, clearly and silently, inside your head, directly to you. Writing is perhaps the greatest of human inventions, binding together people, citizens of distant epochs, who never knew one another. Books break the shackles of time — proof that humans can work magic."

— CARL SAGAN

Writing also changes the writer, or in a team setting, writers. It sparks thinking and clarifies it. Writers are forced to become more specific so that they are understood. Jeff Bezos, Amazon's founder and its CEO for 27 years, preached about narrative writing as an engine for clearer thinking and higher-quality discussions. Narrative writing is story writing and a narrative can be fiction, nonfiction, or a mix of the two. Basically, it is any writing that tells a story through a narrative structure. Wealthy & Wise is a written as a narrative. A list of bullet points, or a PowerPoint presentation, are typically not narrative writing. In 2004, Jeff Bezos banned PowerPoint presentations at future senior team, 'STeam', meetings and replaced them with a well-structured narrative text, four-pages long (later expanded to six-pages). Below is his email.

> "From: Bezos, Jeff
>
> Sent: Wednesday, June 09, 2004 6:02 pm
>
> Subject: Re: No powerpoint presentations from now on at steam
>
> A little more help with the question "why."
>
> Well structured, narrative text is what we're after rather than just text. If someone builds a list of bullet points in word, that would be just as bad as powerpoint.
>
> The reason writing a good 4-page memo is harder than "writing" a 20-page powerpoint is because the narrative

structure of a good memo forces better thought and better understanding of what's more important than what, and how things are related.

Powerpoint-style presentations somehow give permission to gloss over ideas, flatten out any sense of relative importance, and ignore the interconnectedness of ideas."

A top-notch, six-page narrative memo takes time and cannot be written in a few hours or even a day, but the whole process—writing the initial draft, getting feedback from others on how to improve the draft, setting it aside, then restructuring the draft further and so on—promotes better understanding of the ideas and is full of learning for everyone involved in the writing process.

But the inner voice concept is much, much bigger than just a life hack for getting people to listen to your proposals. Our behavior, actions, and results are also consistent with the little voice in our head. Our thought processes are dominated by having unspoken conversations with ourselves. The inner voice is central to how we learn to control ourselves, and it shapes our wellbeing. These unspoken, internal conversations can be constructive as well as destructive.

"The Mind is its own place, and in itself
Can make a Heav'n of Hell, a Hell of Heav'n."
— MILTON, Paradise Lost

I was a freshman at Louisiana State University (LSU) in 1980 and one of the reading assignments was Julian Jaynes' *The Origin of Consciousness in the Breakdown of the Bicameral Mind*. Reading Jaynes' views on how the mind works was jaw-dropping for eighteen-year-old me. Jaynes' solutions touch on many disciplines and his creativity was undeniable. I was not aware of Charlie Munger yet, so it was Jaynes that provided me with my first clear demonstration of the power of utilizing a multi-disciplinary approach, instead of a man-with-a-hammer approach, to reasoning. The detective in Jaynes was undaunted by where the trail led, and he relentlessly followed the evidence (in literature, anthropology, neuroscience, linguistics, psychology, history, religion, and archaeology) to develop his theories. Jaynes provided a spark for me, inspiring me to read more broadly and I continue to be fascinated with the topic. Today, the field has grown bigger, and humanity's knowledge of how the brain works has expanded during the last 40 plus years. However, our understanding of how the human mind works is still at a very early stage. Plenty of discoveries remain to be made.

HUMANS HAVE A STRANGE METHOD FOR PROCESSING INFORMATION

Modern humans have a strange method for processing information that was initially controversial but is well established now. It is important to know—but rarely discussed—that modern humans have two simultaneous operating systems for processing information within their brains. It is like we have two minds in a single brain, and they are often in conflict.

Our ancestors were still largely non-linguistic 200,000 years ago. The human mind back then was more similar to animal minds, consisting of basic animal instincts, needs, and feelings. This ancient, Instinctual Mind is still very much in our heads, very active, and is often our brain's default setting. This Instinctual Mind creates super-fast links that makes rapid judgments below the level of our consciousness, and at times, especially stressful times, our Instinctual Mind can also dominate our inner voice.

As language became more complex and writing developed (less than 6,000 years ago), it altered the human mind. Humanity developed some impactful cognitive upgrades, including the superpowers of reasoning, imagination, and empathy. Much more recently, only about 3,000 years ago, the combination of these superpowers created a highly advanced self-awareness and a new, self-reflective consciousness emerged, which is, in effect, an awareness of the fact that we are aware of ourselves and our actions. With these new superpowers, we were newly capable of contemplating our actions and their consequences.

> *"The Higher Mind is the part of you that can think outside itself and self-reflect and get wiser with experience."*
> — TIM URBAN

Our self-reflective consciousness does not have a material substrate in the brain; it is not hardware. It is more like software that emerged relatively recently in human history, and it runs on our brain (hardware) simultaneously with the Instinctual Mind's ancient animal software. Our understanding of how the human brain processes information is at such an early stage that the labels being used are still dynamic. The varied labels can be confusing. We have both, Thing 1 and Thing 2, in our brain. I will use the label 'Instinctual Mind,' for the portion that developed first and 'Higher Mind' as the label for our self-reflective consciousness that developed much more recently.

- Instinctual Mind: developed earlier and remains active and dominant in humanity's brain today. Many refer to it as our 'unconscious', and you will also hear, 'subconscious and nonconscious' but each of those labels has other, more limited meanings. Albert Einstein referred to having and using two minds and used the label Intuitive Mind for this one. Tim Urban, the writer of the website "Wait buy Why," calls it our Primitive Mind but that can have negative connotations that don't match up with something so powerful, essential, and useful.

- Higher Mind: our self-reflective consciousness that developed much more recently. Jaynes often described our self-reflective consciousness as, 'consciousness.' So do many others, but that word also has other, more limited meanings so it can be a confusing label. Jaynes also called our self-reflective consciousness, "introspective mind space", a descriptive label but it doesn't flow easily off the tongue. Albert Einstein referred to his other mind as his, 'Rational Mind,' and that equates to what Jaynes' would refer to as introspective mind space. Tim Urban, the writer of the website "Wait buy Why," calls it our Higher Mind.

The Instinctual Mind will often be dominant and that can be optimum much of the time and in many situations. The Instinctual Mind is intuitive, powerful, and fast. So fast, you often aren't consciously aware that a decision has been made. However, the Instinctual Mind is prone to biases and is simply not designed to manage long-term risks over decades. Our Instinctual Mind has the instincts and emotions of our hunter-gatherer ancestors and thinks about risks as a short-term phenomenon, the unexpected attack of a predator or an enemy and can react with lightning speed to hide, fight, or run. However, investing successfully is all about long-term phenomenon. The instantaneous instinctual response that serves us well when we are physically attacked can result in buy-high and sell-low behavior in the stock market.

Many of our Instinctual Mind's innate behaviors can be contrary to our investment success (fear, greed, worry, pride, envy, arrogance, boredom, and despair are just a few examples). Learning to think long-term and control your emotions is crucial to successfully investing in stocks. Gaining investing experience will help, but if you continually struggle with either, dollar-cost averaging your savings into low-cost stock market index funds is probably how you should invest in the stock market.

You want to tap the brakes on your fast Instinctual Mind when you invest in stocks because you want your Higher Mind to be predominant. The Higher Mind is slower and more analytical. It is necessary for complex tasks requiring focused attention, but using your Higher Mind for extended periods can be exhausting. That is why after using your Higher Mind it can be efficient to take a break at some point to return later refreshed. Investing in individual stock names can help you develop a more efficient and effective Higher Mind since it provides incentives and countless opportunities to exercise and strengthen your powers of reasoning, imagination, and empathy.

> *"The conscious mind is the editor,*
> *and the subconscious mind is the writer."*
> — STEVE MARTIN

When I was much younger and first started to take notice of my inner voice, I trusted it and thought it was my authentic self. I felt like I should always listen to, believe, and obey what I heard from my inner voice, but I now firmly believe that is a mistake and a big mistake for some people. It is just a voice. It is not your true self. You should be aware of it, but you can take control of your inner voice and change it if it is not being constructive.

With effort, your Higher Mind can override or withstand the instincts, needs, or feelings of your Instinctual Mind. It starts with developing an awareness of both Instinctual and Higher Mind efforts. Your true self can observe both. Each is a state of mind. Neither one fully defines you. Take note when the Instinctual Mind is prominent within your inner voice and know this: unless it is being constructive, you can and should switch your inner voice away from your Instinctual Mind and allow your Higher Mind to drive your behavior.

> *"When observing his own life, a man may often notice*
> *in himself two different beings: the one is blind and physical,*
> *the other sees and is spiritual."*
> — LEO TOLSTOY

The Higher Mind is rational, reasonable, and thoughtful. Being able to place your Higher Mind in the driver's seat of your being is a volitional act— it's a learned skill—and the primary benefit from doing so is that it creates a better foundation for a serenely happy, flourishing, and productive self with less frustration, anxiety, depression, and melancholia. A secondary benefit, a lagniappe, is it will also contribute to your investment success.

It is difficult to describe how tough it can be to control your emotions when the stock market moves against your investments, and you see a large decline in your portfolio's value. We have a hard time predicting how we'll act during future stressful events. We overestimate our intellectual abilities and underestimate our emotional drive. Your Instinctual Mind's impulsivity will activate. You can and should be more than your impulses. To successfully invest, you will need to win the struggle between the

Instinctual Mind's impulsivity and the Higher Mind's self-control. Self-control is just empathy with your future self. A person must be able to see themselves in the future and have empathy for their future self.

"Empathy depends on your ability to overcome your own perspective, appreciate someone else's, and step into their shoes. Self-control is essentially the same skill, except that those other shoes belong to your future self—a removed and hypothetical entity who might as well be a different person. So think of self-control as a kind of temporal selflessness. It's Present You taking a hit to help out Future You."

— ED YONG

Recall that writing, according to Carl Sagan, is "perhaps the greatest of human inventions." Your Higher Mind is intimately tied to language use. Writing can facilitate your effort to maintain self-control and stay rational. Create a habit of writing notes when you decide to buy a stock. Your notes should include the gist of your analysis, the reasons you think it is a good business, and why you purchased the shares. Imagine possible futures. These scenarios can be developed from listing key business metrics or upcoming milestones and deciding what you will do if they change for the good or bad. Then, as a subsequent, separate step, also imagine what you will do after you purchase the stock if the share price goes up, down, or stays flat for each of your scenarios. Jot down the scenarios and how your future self will act.

HOW TO SELECT
THE RIGHT STOCKS

Recall from the buy-and-hold discussion that it will be the quality of the underlying business that you invest in which determines your returns when shares of stock are held for decades. This is true because, over the long term, it's unlikely for a stock to earn a much better return than the business which underlies it earns. This next section, how to choose the right stocks, will therefore be important. It will outline how you can distinguish good businesses from bad ones and how you can take advantage of stock market volatility to gain an edge.

Investment is most intelligent when it is most businesslike.
It is amazing to see how many capable businessmen try to operate in
Wall Street with complete disregard of all the sound principles through
which they have gained success in their own undertakings. Yet every
corporate security may best be viewed, in the first instance, as an
ownership interest in, or a claim against, a specific business enterprise."
— BEN GRAHAM

There are multiple strategies for choosing and investing in stocks but the only approach that I have personally found to be consistently insightful—and of high utility—is the approach outlined in Ben Graham's book, The Intelligent Investor, first published in 1949. I should add that Graham's book was a difficult read for me. I read it in the late 1980s, and it took me a long time to digest. It was the investment in Berkshire Hathaway, that began in 1993, plus continually digesting Warren Buffett's communications over the years that helped me understand Ben Graham's ideas and how to apply them in today's market environment.

The Intelligent Investor defines the big three ideas that should be the cornerstone for your investing:

1. Stocks are just pieces of businesses.
2. View the market, "Mr. Market," as someone there to serve you, not to inform you.
3. Ensure you have a Margin of Safety.

Now let's expand on the three cornerstone ideas.

1. STOCKS ARE JUST PIECES OF BUSINESSES.

You should view buying a stock as more than simply buying a virtual "piece of paper" with a ticker symbol and quoted prices that bounce around, changing constantly, throughout each day. Instead, every share of stock should be seen as an ownership interest in, a very small piece of, an actual business with an underlying intrinsic value that does not depend on its share price in the stock market.

Here is a video clip, https://youtu.be/8OcegOGAGIs?si=XLsqUvDsiRdLKASi, from Warren Buffett's first TV interview, back in 1985. If the link does not work, you can search for the video with, "Warren Buffett 1985 interview Adam Smith Money World." Please watch the video. It is less than 8 minutes long and the video contains a lot of investing insights, simply explained. It is one of Warren's most iconic interviews ever.

Warren is renowned by many as a stock picker, but a key point from the video is that stocks are just pieces of businesses. That means Warren is a business analyst. Like Warren, you must become effective at analyzing businesses to be effective at analyzing stocks.

"Your goal as an investor should simply be to purchase, at a rational price, a part interest in an easily understandable business whose earnings are virtually certain to be materially higher five, ten and twenty years from now. Over time, you will find only a few companies that meet these standards — so when you see one that qualifies, you should buy a meaningful amount of stock. You must also resist the temptation to stray from your guidelines: if you aren't willing to own a stock for ten years, don't even think about owning it for ten minutes. Put together a portfolio of companies whose aggregate earnings march upward over the years, and so also will the portfolio's value."

— WARREN BUFFETT

USEFUL BUSINESS ANALYSIS CAN BE SIMPLE!

The good news is useful business analysis can be simple. Many people already have, or can develop, a basic sense of the merits and faults of business opportunities. That skill set can be effectively applied, or further developed, to enable you to evaluate stocks for potential purchase decisions.

Imagine you wanted to own a pizza parlor. To be clear, the business does not have to be a pizza restaurant. It could be any business venture, privately held or publicly traded on the stock market, including a farm, barber shop, apartment complex, oil production company (ConocoPhillips), conglomerate holding company (Berkshire Hathaway), electric-vehicle maker and technology development company (Tesla), internet commerce company (Amazon), or whatever. For this example, we will imagine a pizza parlor.

A key to investing is learning how to determine your own independently derived value estimate, also known as the intrinsic value of the business. To be clear, the intrinsic value is not dependent on the stock price. Once derived, the intrinsic value may be close to the stock market's view of value, but it also may be different. What you hope to find are intrinsic values that exceed the market's view of value because that provides you with an opportunity to buy the shares of stock in the stock market for less than what you believe the underlying business is worth.

Many businesses, like our imagined pizza business, are not publicly traded. Privately held businesses will not have daily stock market quotes, but their owners can still derive an estimate of the intrinsic value of their businesses. You can apply the same intrinsic value estimating techniques to publicly traded companies as an alternative to the stock market's view of value.

Determining your own independent view of the intrinsic business value may sound difficult, but it does not have to be. Your view of value does not need to be precise. It can and should be a very general estimate, a rough view, about the value of the underlying business. As John Maynard Keynes said, "it's better to be roughly right than precisely wrong." You are looking for cinches, not close calls. Your intent is not precision, not trying to buy businesses worth $82 billion for $79 billion. A precise estimate with that level of accuracy would be an unrealistic expectation and a waste of effort. Being vaguely or roughly right is possible and sufficient in the world of stock investing. Stock investing is uncertain. You should leave yourself a large margin for error, a margin of safety.

Let us therefore consider how to determine the intrinsic value for an operating business. We will start with an imaginary pizza business and then turn to actual investments that were made in the real-world. The real-world examples will start with a well-established mature business without a lot of growth potential and then we will look at a couple of earlier-stage, higher growth business examples. Determining the underlying business's intrinsic value will be covered first and then that will be followed by how to find the stock market's value (using the stock's share price) as an alternative value estimate.

A LIFE HACK FOR VALUING STOCKS

You could look at lots and lots of variables, but what matters to determine a business's value is understanding the cash flow. More specifically, the amount of cash the business can return to its owners over time, from now through the future.

"Cash...is to a business as oxygen is to an individual: never thought about when it is present, the only thing in mind when it is absent."
— WARREN BUFFETT

Our imagined pizza restaurant may be crowded every day, the food may be delicious, the atmosphere charming, and millions of other attractive things, but a mature business that is not capable of producing positive cash flow—money that can be put into the owners' pocket—is not operating well as a business.

When people hear the words cash flow, they may think of complicated balance sheets, financial statements, and so on. They may wonder how they are going to tell the difference between all the confusing numbers. Or, they might have a flashback to college finance and accounting. Some people may consider these things boring or difficult, but here is a simple methodology to help you think about and analyze the cash flow of mature businesses. It is a mental model, or a "Life Hack," that I refer to as "Business as a Box," and it makes understanding cashflow and calculating intrinsic value easier. It has been a useful way to think about businesses and potential decisions to buy or sell stocks in a publicly traded company.

Business as a Box reveals how well a business is operating, and when you combine that with Ben Graham's insight that you should evaluate stocks in the same way you evaluate a business, "Business as a Box" will yield two equivalent mental models: one for businesses and one for the corresponding stock.

Here is how to apply the business as a box mental model. Start by imagining a box and an owner. In the image below, it looks like a regular box. You may be wondering why the owner is smiling. Why is she happy about owning what appears to be a regular box?

Owner

Well, it is not a regular box; it is a magical box that can spit out cash for its owner year after year for many years with no degradation over time in the magical box's cash-creation capability. The owner can put the cash that comes out of the box in her pocket or allocate it to whatever she wishes.

Cash Available for Owner

Owner

Such a box would be great to own. An owner, or owners, could also easily calculate the box's intrinsic value: the sum of the present values of future cash that will be produced over time, and they could easily evaluate the merits of any buy or sell offers. If someone offers to buy your box for a lot less money than what will come out of the box, you will know that selling the box does not make financial sense for you.

When you look at a mature business, imagine what it would take for the business of interest to be equivalent to a box that can spit out cash for its owner (or owners) year after year, for many years, with no degradation over time in the business's cash-creation capability.

The imagined pizza business is named Bella's. It sells finished products (pizzas) creating revenue. The main operating expenses will be ingredients (flour, tomatoes, cheese, toppings, and so on) and running the restaurant (rent, electricity, employee salaries, taxes, and so on). The revenue minus expenses will generate Bella's cashflow from operating activities. And from time to time, Bella's will incur other costs (replacing ovens, updating decor, and so on) to ensure no degradation in the business over time. After accounting for all their revenue and operating expenses and after deducting additional amounts to allow for the cash that would be required to ensure no decline in the scale or quality of the business over time, Bella's owners estimate their business can generate roughly $500,000 of positive cashflow (cashflow from operating activities minus capital expenditures), in today's dollars, for them year after year.

This $500,000 per year estimate is the cash available for owners after sustaining the current state of the business. It is how much cash you, as the owner, can withdraw from the business each year without hurting the business's current or long-term prospects. The amounts you can withdraw each year without degrading the business is a normalized annual cash available for owners estimate in real dollars. The annual cash available for owners has been normalized to a no-growth and no-decline business state future scenario. The business's actual annual cash available for owners may be different, for example, annual amounts available for owners will be less in the near-term when the business is investing to grow.

What is the intrinsic value of Bella's pizza business? If you thought the business will continue to be run equally well in the future, you could pay $10 million to purchase Bella's and earn a 5% real annual return. You could withdraw $500,000 per year of cash on average without hurting the business's current or long-term prospects and $0.5 million divided by $10 million is 5% each year. If you paid $5 million to purchase Bella's, you could earn a 10% real annual return ($0.5 million divided by $5 million). If you paid $3 million, you could earn a 15% real annual return ($0.5 million divided by $3.3 million is 15%).

Your intrinsic value calculation depends on your return expectations. If you assume inflation will be roughly 3% on average, add 3% to the real returns to determine nominal returns. Your return expectations are also called discount rates. The table below has a valuation summary for Bella's.

Value (potential purchase price)	Annual Nominal / Real Return Expectations, (Discount Rate)
$10 million	8% / 5%
$5 million	13% / 10%
$3 million	18% / 15%

Further imagine you have $10 million available. How much would you be willing to pay for the pizza business? If you paid $10 million for Bella's, your 8% nominal (5% real) annual return expectation from the business investment would be about what you could expect from passively investing in a low-cost stock market index fund, but an investment in the index fund would require almost no effort from you. If you could purchase Bella's for only $3 million, your 18% nominal (15% real) return would be much better, more than double what you could expect from passive investments in the stock market.

As a very general rule of thumb for stock investments in mature publicly traded businesses, I usually consider a business valuation to be reasonable if a normalized annual cash available for owners' estimate yields a real return of 5%. A Business as a Box outcome with a 10% real return is an attractive (low-priced) valuation for stock investments. So, for me, Bella's is likely worth $5-10 million, if you believed the business will be run equally well in the future. The assumption at the end of the sentence, 'the business will be run equally well in the future,' is important. Obviously, you would have higher expected returns if you paid the lowest possible amount when the estimated business results are the same for each case.

You will often hear that the value of a business—your independently derived intrinsic business value—is the sum of the present values of all future cash flows that the business can be expected to generate for its owner: the present values of all the cash available for owners from that business. The key idea behind present values is that the further in the future a cash flow occurs, the less it is worth to you today. The mathematical method is called discounted cash flow analysis and that is how you should determine the intrinsic value of a business, whether the business is privately held or publicly traded. Discounted cash flow analysis calculates the present value of expected future cash flows using a discount rate (a return expectation). The pizza business example is discounted cash flow analysis: the normalized cash available for owners estimate, the annual cash flow of $500,000, in real dollars, is 'discounted' by the various return expectations (5, 10 and 15%) to yield each of the business values shown (10, 5 or $3 million).

Below is Warren Buffett's description of discounted cash flow analysis, copied from his 2000 letter to Berkshire Hathaway shareholders:

"Leaving aside tax factors, the formula we use for evaluating stocks and businesses is identical. Indeed, the formula for valuing all assets that are purchased for financial gain has been unchanged since it was first laid out by a very smart man in about 600 BC (though he wasn't smart enough to know it was 600 BC). The oracle was Aesop and his enduring, though somewhat incomplete, investment insight was 'a bird in the hand is worth two in the bush.

To flesh out this principle, you must answer only three questions,

1. *How certain are you that there are indeed birds in the bush?*

2. *When will they emerge and how many will there be?*

3. *What is the risk-free interest rate (which we consider to be the yield on long-term US bonds)?"*

If you can answer these three questions, you will know the maximum value of the bush—and the maximum number of the birds you now possess that should be offered for it. And, of course, don't literally think birds. Think dollars.

"Aesop's investment axiom, thus expanded and converted into dollars, is immutable. It applies to outlays for farms, oil royalties, bonds, stocks, lottery tickets, and manufacturing plants. And neither the advent of the steam engine, the harnessing of electricity, nor the creation of the automobile changed the formula one iota (not even the Internet). Just insert the correct numbers, and you can rank the attractiveness of all possible uses of capital throughout the universe."

It is important to recognize that your normalized annual cash available for owners estimate that is derived from Business as a Box is a possible future scenario. It is useful because having a normalized annual estimate simplifies the discounted cash flow calculation. The Business as a Box outcome also creates a conservative base case scenario in real dollars, with no volume growth but also no degradation in the business size nor quality over time. That base case, of no growth and no decline, can be used to compare against other alternative cash flow scenarios. Two obvious alternative scenarios would be that the managers could 1.) decide to spend more money in the business, by reinvesting a portion of the normalized annual cash available for owners or by raising money, to try to grow the business over time, or 2.) could spend less money in the business (use cheaper ingredients, reduce staff, cut advertising expenses, and so on), to increase the amount of cash available for owners in the near-term, and accept that the business's scale or quality may diminish over time.

When you determine the value of a publicly traded business using discounted cash flow analysis, you have derived an estimate of the intrinsic business value of that stock name and your estimate is independent of its current stock price. Bella's, as a privately owned business, would not even have a stock price. Even though publicly traded businesses have a quoted stock price, you do not use the stock price when you estimate the intrinsic business value. After you independently derive an intrinsic value for the business, you will then compare your value estimate to the stock market's valuation of the same business. The stock market's valuation is derived from the stock price. How to find the stock market's valuation will be covered in the next section.

The business as a box and discounted cash flow analysis methodologies can be, and should be, applied to evaluate the merits of larger, more complex businesses. For example, ConocoPhillips is a publicly traded business that produces and sells oil and natural gas. It is a mature business with limited growth potential. You would be reasonable to expect a mature business with limited growth potential like ConocoPhillips to be able to return cash to shareholders (owners). Let's apply the business as a box methodology to ConocoPhillips.

What magic needs to be in the box for ConocoPhillips?

CASHFLOW FROM OPERATIONS AND CAPITAL INTENSITY

At a high level, we need the same two numbers we used in the pizza business: cashflow from operating activities and capital intensity. Cashflow from operating activities is the amount of money a company generates from ongoing, regular business activities, such as manufacturing and selling goods (for example, barrels of oil or delicious pizzas) or providing a service. Cashflow from operating activities does not include cashflow from investing activities nor from financing activities. Profitable cashflow from operating activities is a positive thing for owners; the bigger it is the better.

Capital intensity is not an accounting term, but it is all important and can be found, or figured out, if you know to look for it. Capital Intensity is how much cash ConocoPhillips needs to spend each year on average to sustain their current state for many years—the money that ConocoPhillips needs to spend on average annually just to keep production flat at current levels and without allowing any degradation to their portfolio's quality. Capital intensity is a cost and a negative thing for owners; the smaller it is the better.

Cashflow from operations is relatively easy to find; it will be disclosed with the financials in quarterly earnings calls and in annual reports published by the company. To figure out capital intensity, you need to do a bit more detective work. But once you have the "business as a box" model inside your head, you will notice lots of references to what I am calling capital intensity. Listen to the answers provided to questions from analysts during the quarterly calls. You will have to listen to the management of the company, but also test what they say by looking at the actual operating results over time, applying judgement or contingency to determine your own view of the capital intensity.

Below are a few examples of capital intensity from ConocoPhillips' earning calls:

"... we can keep production flat for over a decade with capex of $5 billion to $6 billion." — Ryan Lance, CEO, during July 28, 2016, ConocoPhillips Earnings Call, page 4 of transcript

"Expected production growth of 4% in 2018 with capital spend of $6 billion." — Ryan Lance, April 26, 2018, in the first quarter of 2018 Earnings call

"Sustain near-term production with $3.5 billion of capital per year plus near-term funding for exploration and major projects of $0.8 billion per year." — May 2018, Update to 2017 Analysts and Investors

You may have noticed from those earnings call comments that ConocoPhillips' capital intensity may have been improving during the period of the earnings—a rare and wonderful thing that improves the profitability outlook and a good sign that the business is performing well.

Capital Intensity

At the end of 2019, you could have estimated that ConocoPhillips needed to spend $4 billion each year to sustain their current state for many years—$4 billion a year is the capital intensity of ConocoPhillips at the start of 2020. The average, annual amount of capital (cash) that ConocoPhillips will need to re-invest into the existing business just to keep production flat at current levels and without allowing any material degradation to their existing assets is estimated at about $4 billion each year.

If $4 billion a year sounds high, it is, but if ConocoPhillips decided to spend less than $4 billion a year, current production levels will gradually decline in the future. Oil and gas production companies, and many other businesses, are very capital intensive, much more capital intensive than what it would take to maintain a successful pizza business. To be fair, a pizza parlor will have plenty of challenges too, but capital intensity is not likely to be the pizza restaurant's biggest business issue. Another point to highlight is that ConocoPhillips' actual spending was more than $4 billion a year at the time since their intent was to deliver a modest level of overall business growth, and they were investing additional capital to deliver that modest level of growth.

What comes out of the box for ConocoPhillips? The difference between cashflow from operating activities and capital intensity will be the normalized annual cash available for owners—the cash available for owners after sustaining the current state, or if retained by the business and not paid out to owners, that amount could be used to grow the business, repurchase shares, pay down debt, and so on (cash has many possible uses).

ConocoPhillips sells its products (oil and gas) at prices outside of its control and will create much higher levels of cash from operations when oil prices are high and lower levels when oil prices are low, but oil and gas valuations should be based on average prices over the long-term. Oil prices are quite volatile in the short-term, but the estimate for long-term average oil prices is much more stable at about $60 per Brent barrel in real terms (2020 dollars) and would be closer to $70 in 2024 dollars after adjusting the real amount for inflation (60 multiplied by 1.03 four times).

ConocoPhillips Cash Available for Owners or for Growth with 2019 Performance

+ Cash from Operations Sensitivities

Brent Oil Price ($/Bbl)	Annual CFO ($ billions)
40	5.2
50	7.9
60	10.6
70	13.3
80	16.0

- Capital Intensity
  - ~$4 billion/year, to sustain current state for many years
  - Capital to keep production flat plus minimal capital projects, exploration and business development

- Cash available for owners or, if retained by the business, for growth
  - Cash from operations minus capital intensity

Brent Oil Price ($/Bbl)	Cash Available for Owners or Growth ($ billions)
40	1.2
50	3.9
60	6.6
70	9.3
80	12.0

$10.6 billion of annual cash flow from operations and $6.6 billion of cash available for owners or for growth with 2019 performance and $60 Brent

The model predicted that ConocoPhillips at the beginning of 2020 could ensure no degradation to current production levels for many years and create about $6.6 billion per year of cash (in 2020 dollars) for owners or for growth if oil prices averaged $60 per real Brent barrel. Recall that your intrinsic value estimate depends on your return expectations. The annual $6.6 billion of normalized cash available for owners is 'discounted' by the various return expectations (5, 10, 15 and 20%) to yield each of the business value estimates shown in the table below (132, 66, 44 or $33 billion).

Value	Annual Nominal / Real Return Expectation
$132 billion	8% / 5%
$66 billion	13% / 10%
$44 billion	18% / 15%
$33 billion	23% / 20%

Recall that Business as a Box creates a conservative business case with the level of business reinvestment constrained to a no volume growth scenario. For me, ConocoPhillips at the beginning of 2020 was likely to be worth a range of $70-130 billion. If you paid $130 billion to buy all the shares, you could expect to earn a 5% real return over the long-term. If you paid $70 billion you could expect to earn a 10% real return. If you want a single number, you could take the midpoint of $100 billion, but it is useful to remember that intrinsic valuations are rough, not precise, estimates.

Therefore, based on the model and discounted cashflow analysis, if you could purchase all of ConocoPhillips for $100 billion at the beginning of 2020, you could expect to earn about a 10% nominal and 7% real annual return in the future based on a $60 real Brent average oil price forecast and no business volume growth in the future. You will compare your intrinsic value estimate of $100 billion to the stock market's value, and we will cover how to find the stock market's value in the next section. Valuations by the stock market as high as $130 billion would be reasonable (not cheap but not expensive) and valuations that are at the lower end of the valuation range, values below a $100 billion, would be a buying opportunity. Obviously, you would have higher expected returns if you paid the lowest possible amount.

In contrast to the large ConocoPhillips' value estimates above, you would probably be surprised how many times you will find companies that are highly valued by the stock market but that need to re-invest almost all their positive cashflow back into the business just to maintain their current state—with a no growth and no decline case, those businesses will generate no or limited annual cash available for owners (amazing what the business as a box methodology reveals). A business that does not grow nor have cash available for owners is not adding real value (assuming flat, real product prices); if you paid a fair-value price one year and sold it five years later at a fair-value price, you would have no real value gains after adjusting for inflation. You want the opposite of that, you want real value gains, to occur after you buy stocks.

You should track "Business as a Box" results over time to monitor business performance and valuation trends. Your intrinsic value estimates will help you stay focused on what matters, business performance, and the process gets easier over time as you hold your shares. Intrinsic value estimates generally change only gradually, unlike stock market valuations, which can change quickly and significantly each time the stock price jiggles up or down. You can also apply the model to industry competitors to identify top performers and so on. Overall, the simple "Business as a Box" model can yield insightful and useful results.

HOW TO SPOT HIGH-QUALITY GROWING BUSINESSES

Let's return to Bella's pizza business and add to the story. The owners are Angelo and his daughter Sophia. The restaurant's namesake, Bella, was the beloved wife of Angelo and mother of Sophia. It was Bella's restaurant, but she died unexpectedly shortly after the restaurant opened ten years ago. When her mom died Sophia quit university to keep the restaurant with her dad. Angelo and Sophia jointly own and run Bella's. Both love the business.

It has been ten years, but Angelo still imagines he is creating each menu item for Bella. As he has gained experience, he has become a culinary artist. Sophia, always clever, has learned the restaurant business well and has become the leader of everything else necessary for a successful business. Sophia has become brilliant at turning her dad's delicious ideas into profitable products. Sophia is also motivated and inspired by vivid memories of her mom. Bella died years ago, but it is still Bella's restaurant. Both know Bella would be very proud of what they have done with the business, although it has been hard for them to talk about Bella with each other.

Bella's is very popular, not just for the Pizzas. Angelo now regularly adds limited edition special entrees to the menu that are all the rage. The current business is operating extremely well based on almost every metric. Customers love the food, the atmosphere, and the service. The employees enjoy being a part of a well-run, popular business and are happy working at Bella's. Most importantly, Sophia knows well that the cash available for owners as a percentage of total sales (a type of profit margin) is in the top quartile, or higher, of the restaurant industry.

The only business issue is growth. Bella's is a relatively small business, a single venue in a major city, and the business is operating at full capacity.

With her dad, they have fully optimized her mom's original vision for the restaurant. In wanting to honor her mom's memory, Sophia realizes they have been too reluctant to make changes that would enable the business to grow, and Bella's cannot expand further unless they make some big changes.

Sophia decided to focus on all the bottlenecks in their current business without constraining herself to Bella's current footprint and processes. Sophia was pleasantly surprised that each opportunity became interesting when she investigated them deeply enough. She also learned the meaning of, 'a problem well-stated is half-solved.' (Charles Kettering). Sophia's efforts also enabled her to more fully recall that her mom had been an excellent problem solver. When she mentioned that to her dad, it was a cathartic release. They stayed up for hours talking about her mom; it was a conversation that both needed but had been emotionally unable to do before. Sophia quickly identified lots of growth opportunities.

One constraint to growth was it would cost a lot of money. Sophia focused on how to optimize the scope and schedule and was able to reduce the initial cost estimate a lot. What she ultimately defined was a growth plan that would take 3 years and cost an incremental investment of $1 million. When the growth plan was implemented, the business could triple — normalized cash available for owners would go from the current $500,000 per year to $1.5 million a year on a real dollar's basis after about three years.

Sophia's excitement was contagious. Angelo caught it. They discussed how to fund the growth plan. Bella's business success had not gone unnoticed. Two people were particularly ardent to provide funding: 1.) Jake, a well-dressed, smooth talking, private equity investor, and 2.) Alastair, a grim local banker.

Each proposal is summarized below:

1.) Private Equity: Jake wanted to contribute $1 million to fund the growth plan, not charge any interest at all, but he wanted to own a one-third share of the business in exchange.

Paying no interest was attractive to Sophia at first mention (Jake said "Zero Interest" a lot!) but giving up a third of the business meant giving up $500,000 annually from the expanded business for the life of the business (one third of the $1.5 million a year of normalized cash available for owners is $500,000 annually). Jake argued that a third of the current free cashflow available for owners from the business was less than $170,000 a year (one third of only $0.5 million) and that would yield a 17% real annual return on his $1 million investment. Sophia correctly identified that Jake's returns would soon grow to 50% a year on his $1 million investment once the growth plan was implemented. Sophia was confident her expansion would work. Sophia felt Jake's offer was much too expensive. Plus, Jake did not seem interested in being a long-term owner. Jake never explicitly said so, but Sophia sensed that he would want to sell the business or at least his share once the growth plan was implemented. Sophia decided she wasn't keen on adding a new owner. Angelo was also uneasy about Jake and about the idea of having Jake constantly around. Angelo quickly agreed with Sophia that they should not add a new owner.

2.) Bank Loan: Alastair's bank was willing to loan them money to expand the business. Sophia and Angelo would pay back the loan amount of $1 million over 10 years plus pay a 12.5% nominal annual interest rate. Their payments to the bank would be $180,000 a year, a cumulative $1.8 million over 10 years, almost doubling the cost of Sophia's growth plan. The total interest paid would be a cumulative $0.8 million during the 10 years.

Sophia and Angelo could retain full ownership of Bella's and have access to 100% of future cash available for owners if they used a bank loan. However, as Sophia pondered Alastair's proposal, she began to realize that during the loan payback period the bank would basically be a business partner. The bank, as the debtholder, would even get paid before the shareholders (Angelo and Sophia each own a half share in Bella's) could withdraw any cash available for owners. The bank payments would also reduce the overall amount of cash available for owners. Taking the bank loan would be equivalent to creating a time-limited partnership with Alastair and his bank. Not forever, but 10 years would be a long time. Although the bank loan would provide funding, and it would be much cheaper than Jake's proposal, the thought of Alastair as even a time-limited partner was not appealing. Sophia was keenly interested in finance but whenever she tried learning from Alastair, he was curt and condescending. Alastair's primary comments to Sophia were wanting to know if her dad was available to talk with him. Furthermore, Alastair on no occasion ate at Bella's, not before and not even when they would meet at Bella's, with food offered, to discuss funding. Alastair was a dour, numbers guy. He seemed joyless when doing almost anything. A 10-year business relationship with Alastair would still be expensive, with $0.8 million of interest payments, and no fun.

Sophia briefly wondered why any business would issue shares or take on debt to expand their business. Many businesses do not have a choice. A start-up business, for example, needs to raise capital or have money already saved to fund its early years while ramping up the business to profitable levels. Ramping up to profitable levels can take time. Other businesses may be more mature than a startup, but very many, are just not profitable enough; they consume almost all the cash available to simply maintain the current business with no cash left over for real growth.

Bella's, however, is no longer a startup. Although it is relatively small, Bella's is a high-quality business that generates high profit margins. Sophia realizes correctly that Bella's had been built strong enough to self-fund the $1 million growth plan. Bella could organically grow their business by eliminating cash withdrawals from owners for 2 years or, alternatively, reduce the withdrawals to $170,000 per year for three years.

Either reduction would allow an incremental $1 million to be reinvested into the business to fund Sophia's growth plan without raising any debt nor selling equity (there would be no need to issue new shares that would dilute existing owners).

When a portion of the normalized annual cash available for owners is retained by the business, instead of being paid out to owners, that retained cash can be reinvested to grow the business organically, without having to raise debt or equity from new parties. High-quality growing businesses can grow and still generate free cash flow. Free cash flow is cash flow from operations minus capital investments. The Business as a Box methodology normalizes the free cash flow estimate to a no-growth and no-decline business case scenario. The annual free cash flow estimate for a growth business case scenario will be lower in the near-term than for a no-growth and no-decline scenario, but free cash flow can still be positive if it is a high-quality growing business. For example, Bella's could triple the size of its business over three years, a 44% compound annual growth rate during those three years, and still generate free cash flow of $170,000 per year.

When you see a growing business, one of the things to look at is the number of shares and the debt levels over an extended period. If the share count and debt levels are stable or, even better, declining and the business is growing at a good growth rate, that is likely to be a high-quality growing business. A business may be able to grow at a faster rate if they raise money externally but the best constraint on growth is that it be profitable.

A high-quality growing business, that is no longer a start-up, should be able to self-fund its growth and still grow at a good rate.

Recall that what matters when determining a business's intrinsic value is cash flow. As an investor, you should focus on what matters (the sources and uses of cash) when assessing business value.

A business's primary sources of cash include cashflow from operating activities (also called operating cash flow), raising debt, and issuing (selling) new shares (increasing the number of shares). A good to wonderful, mature business, like Bella's, can source cash from their existing profitable operating activities, not just to maintain the existing business's current size but also to grow their business over time.

When you focus on cashflow from operating activities, look for trends. Operating cash flow is not static. High demand can allow the business to sell their products at higher prices, that would increase business revenue. Product costs can decrease when productivity improves. Both would be a positive trend and the opposite would be a negative for shareholders. As a real-world example, when comparing 2019 performance to 2016, ConocoPhillips made changes to its portfolio of producing wells that improved the cash from operations (operating cash flow) generated per barrel of oil produced by 36%, after adjusting to constant product prices, (reference the image below); this is a very positive trend for shareholders.

Let's use what we covered so far with Bella's and ConocoPhillips to also make a few general points about possible uses of cash.

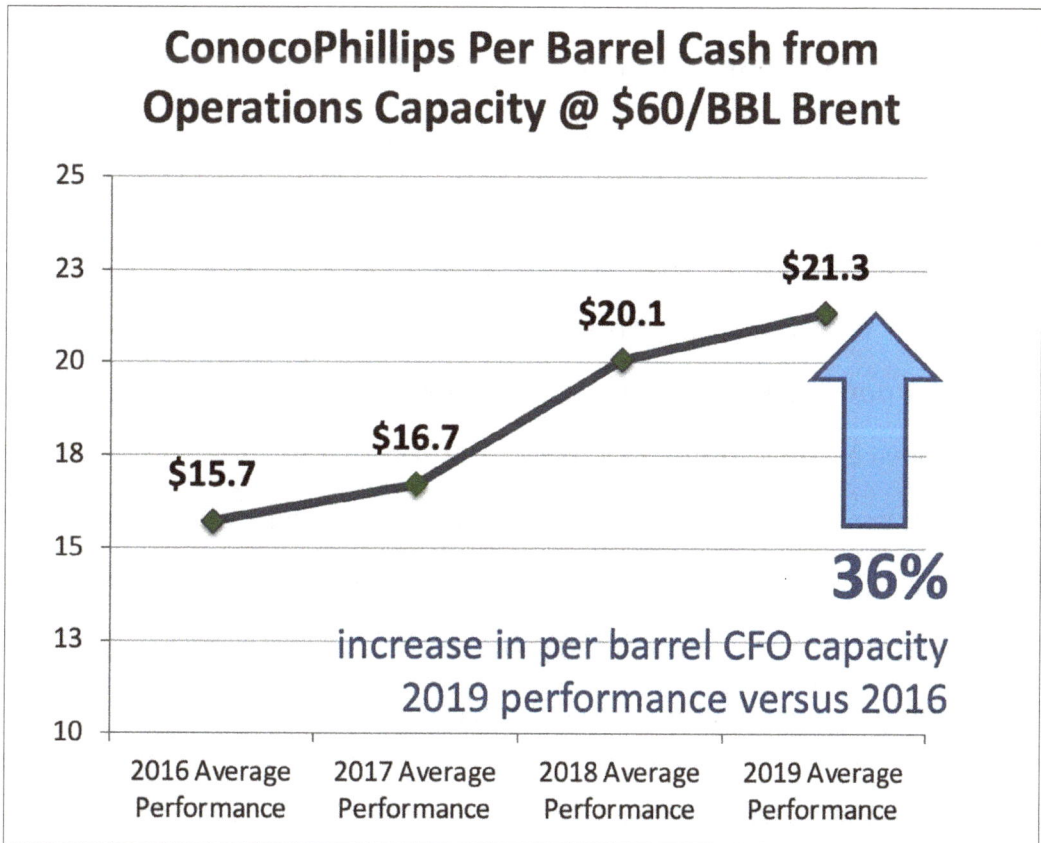

ConocoPhillips Per Barrel Cash from Operations Capacity @ $60/BBL Brent

- $15.7 — 2016 Average Performance
- $16.7 — 2017 Average Performance
- $20.1 — 2018 Average Performance
- $21.3 — 2019 Average Performance

36% increase in per barrel CFO capacity 2019 performance versus 2016

Any of the following eight uses of cash can be beneficial to shareholders, but not under all conditions, and the priority depends on the attractiveness of each one for a given business at a given time. You will need to understand the context to assess the best uses of cash. The best way to get the context is to go to the primary source. Focus on what management says in their earnings calls, annual reports, presentations, and other company material. You should still think independently, remain skeptical, test what they say by looking at the actual operating results over time, and then ultimately determine your own view.

1. Non-discretionary investments (items required to stay in compliance with laws and regulations).

2. Maintain current business state: Invest enough in the business to maintain the business size and quality over time.

3. Pursue organic growth: grow the business by re-investing into the existing business when attractive opportunities exist.

4. Pay a dividend to shareholders (owners).

5. Pay down debt especially when it is expensive, or the business has an excessive amount.

6. Repurchase shares when the stock price is undervalued or at the least not overvalued relative to the intrinsic value of the business.

7. Acquire other companies to grow the business.

8. Build up cash on the balance sheet.

Capital Intensity investments include both Cash Use 1 and 2. The Business as a Box outcome already incorporates the capital intensity funding prior to estimating a normalized annual cashflow for owners. For example, Bella's $500,000 per year and ConocoPhillips $6.6 billion per year estimates are after-funding capital intensity requirements. Capital intensity is likely to be low for Bella's, but it consumed 40% of ConocoPhillips operating cash flow ($4 billion a year of capital intensity divided by $10.6 billion of operating cash flow per year is 40%). Many other businesses are capital intensive. Capital intensity is a cost, a negative for owners. The lower the amounts that must be allocated to Cash Uses 1 and 2, the better the business. The good news for ConocoPhillips is that their capital intensity trend improved (reduced) from 2016 through 2019 and that improving trend is a good thing.

As an occasional replacement for Cash Use 2, it can make sense at certain times or for some businesses to not reinvest at the levels necessary to maintain the current size of the business. When re-investment opportunities become financial unattractive (with unacceptably low returns on the investment) it is better to decrease reinvestment levels in the existing business to below capital intensity levels and allow the business to shrink or decline over time. An example would be if you owned a business that sold encyclopedias door to door when the internet developed; that business would have started a steady decline and the best outcome could be to harvest as much cash from the business as possible until it reaches a new lower and stable level or it reaches a level so small that it makes sense to exit from or close the business. Businesses that are shrinking can be mispriced by the stock market. Some investors specialize in this category but not generally as a buy-and-hold type, more of a shorter term, investment (held potentially for years but not decades).

For Cash Use 3, ideally, you want to find businesses that are loaded with financially attractive organic growth opportunities since this use of cash typically has by far the highest risk-adjusted returns. Sophia's growth plan is an organic growth plan, has very attractive economics and should be a top funding priority. A two-thirds portion of the normalized cash available for owners ($330,000 per year) can be reinvested for 3 years and that will triple Bella's business value by year 4. ConocoPhillips was not growing its business in the few years prior to 2020. ConocoPhillips' had limited organic growth opportunities at the time, and they wisely used the normalized cash available for owners to pay dividends, repurchase shares, and pay down debt. Each of those alternative uses of cash, and not re-investing at unattractive rates to grow organically, were beneficial at the time to ConocoPhillips shareholders.

Owners would want Bella's to fund more and similar organic growth opportunities to Sophia's growth plan, but since nothing else organic currently exists, it makes sense to payout the remaining normalized cash available for owners to the shareholders as a dividend, Cash Use 4. Bella's dividend distributions could be $170,000 a year (1/3 of $500,000) for three years and could then increase significantly once the growth plan was completed after year 3. Paying dividends is generally a positive thing for shareholders, but it can indicate that the business lacks financially attractive organic growth opportunities. That could indicate the business will be growing at a modest rate in the future.

Paying down debt, Cash Use 5, could be the number one priority when debt levels are excessive, especially so for Sophia if the lender would be Alastair, but Bella's is debt-free. ConocoPhillips paid down its debt level 50% from the start of 2016 through 2018. Interest paid on debt is a cost that reduces the level of operating cash flow: Less debt, less cost, higher operating cash flow. Higher levels of operating cash flow are a good thing.

ConocoPhillips' Improving Debt Levels

$29.5 billion

15.0 billion

Debt Levels (Billions USD)

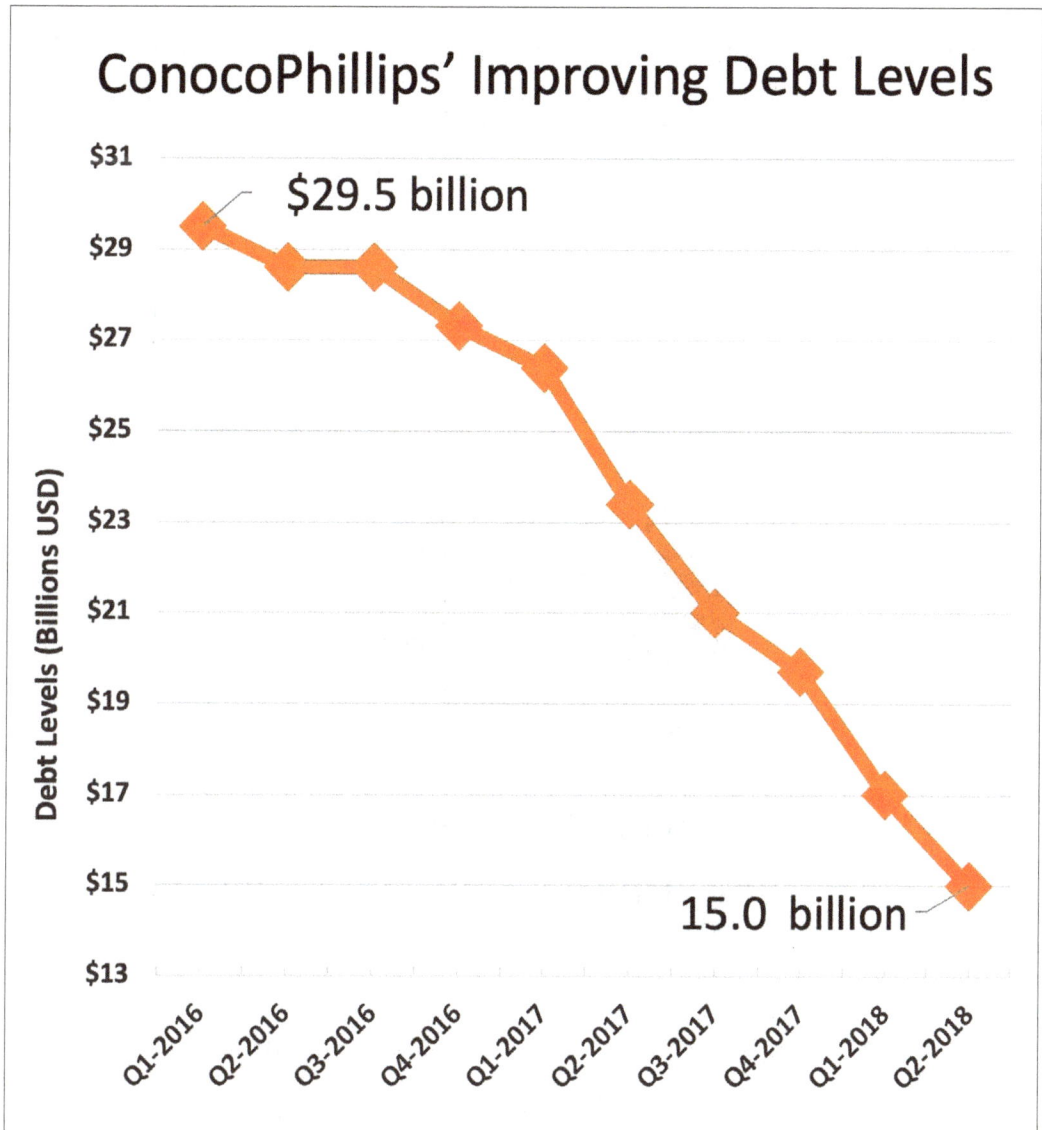

Cash Use 6, stock buybacks (also called share repurchases), can be a very positive thing for shareholders. Buybacks confuse many people, even many business executives. To understand buybacks, instead of imagining the business as a box for a moment, imagine it as a delicious pizza. Recall that every share of stock is an ownership interest in, a very small slice of, an actual business with an underlying value. If you own shares, a decreasing share count for the same size business results in you having a bigger slice of the business. If the total share count decreases by 14% over a period, and you retain your shares, your portion of the business grew by 14% even if the overall business stayed the same size. Your results are even better if the business also grows while the share count decreases and your share increases.

When you can cut fewer slices, decreasing share count, there is more pizza per slice

One concern that is too often ignored is that many companies repurchase shares regardless of the stock price. Value is destroyed when stock purchases are made above the business's intrinsic value and that applies to stock buybacks as well. It is useful to remember that the stock price matters when companies do buybacks.

Buybacks when the stock price is below the business's intrinsic value can be wonderful for shareholders. ConocoPhillips used share repurchases to reduce its share count from 1.25 billion shares of stock at the start of 2016 to 1.08 billion by the end of the first quarter 2020. That is a 14% reduction in share count. If you, as a shareholder, held a constant amount of shares during that period, your share, your slice of the business, increased by 14% in about 4 years.

> *"When companies with outstanding businesses and comfortable financial positions find their shares selling far below intrinsic value in the marketplace, no alternative action can benefit shareholders as surely as repurchases".*
> — WARREN BUFFETT

Bella's only shareholders are Angelo and Sophia. Imagine, at some point, Angelo wishes to retire and sell his share of the business. They could decide to increase the total share count to whatever number they wished. Let's assume they increase the share count to 100, with 50 shares allocated to both Angelo and Sophia initially. Bella's could spend a portion of the annual normalized cash available for owners to gradually purchase shares, with only Angelo, not Sophia selling shares. Over time, as Angelo sold his shares the total share count would decrease. Sophia would retain her 50 shares; Sophia's share of the business would grow, and Angelo would get paid for his original portion of the business. When there are only 50 shares still outstanding, Sophia will own 100% of the business instead of half. Sophia's per share value would increase even if the overall business value remained constant.

Moving on to Cash Use 7, some companies grow by making frequent acquisitions. Adding shareholder value from growth through acquisitions is challenging. Most good businesses sell at elevated prices. I prefer companies that can grow organically. Berkshire Hathaway is an exception; they have a good track record over more than 50 years of making successful acquisitions, but that is rare. Berkshire is the only business in the buy-and-hold collection that frequently relies on acquisitions to grow their overall business. Bella's is not considering acquisitions.

Operating cash flow can also be allowed to build up as cash on the company's balance sheet, Cash Use 8, when the annual operating cash flow is not fully allocated to the other uses. The debt held by a company minus any cash held by the company is referred to as their net-debt. For example, ConocoPhillips had $8 billion of cash and short-term investments on its balance sheet at the end of 2019 and had a debt level of $15 billion, net-debt was $7 billion (15 minus 8). The optimum level of cash to have on the balance sheet varies depending on the business and its situation.

So, if a business is retaining cash to re-invest with financially attractive returns to deliver organic growth of the business, like a pizza business reinvesting a portion of the normalized cash available for owners from its current business to expand for example, you as an owner may be okay with it. You would not be receiving cash distributions (dividends) now, or they may be less than they could be, but you would be able to say, "Look at the size of my business; it is growing fast, getting huge, and at some point, in the future, it will have even more cash available to distribute to owners from an expanded business rather than taking the cash now." Pain now for, perhaps, a larger gain later. If that is the case, it is best when the box (the business) can grow organically, by simply reinvesting positive cashflows from operating activities that are being created internally from the core business.

Sometimes, too often, businesses grow by borrowing money (raising debt) or selling more shares in the existing business. Raising debt or issuing additional shares can sometimes be justified, but the existing owners' portion of the business gets diluted. When that happens, you will want to understand what your portion of the bigger business will be: If the business is growing but your share is shrinking due to dilution when the business raised cash by selling more shares or increasing its debt, that may not be a good thing for you.

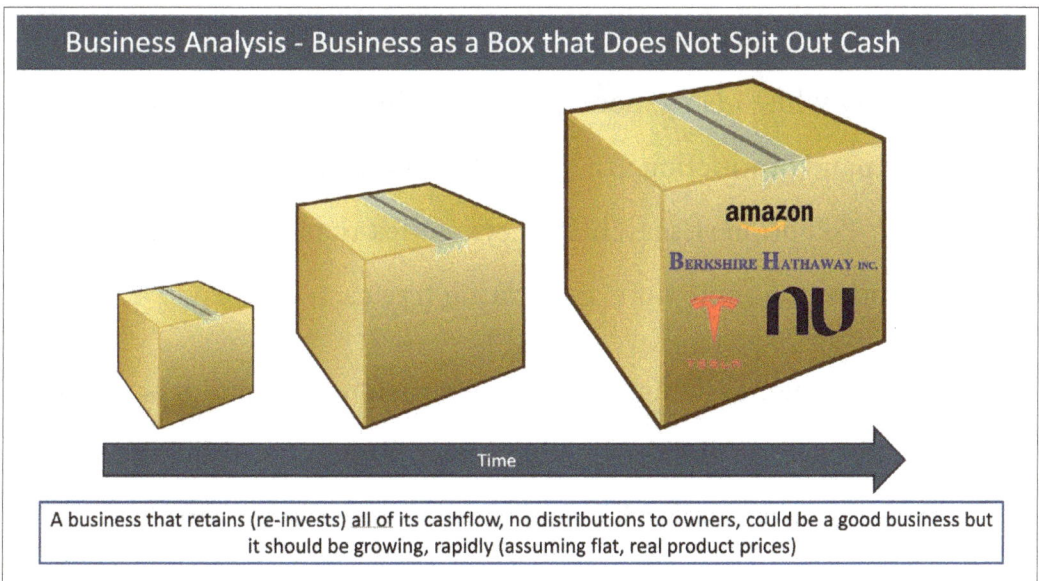

Business Analysis - Business as a Box that Does Not Spit Out Cash

A business that retains (re-invests) all of its cashflow, no distributions to owners, could be a good business but it should be growing, rapidly (assuming flat, real product prices)

Furthermore, not all reinvestment funded growth is intelligent. The reinvestment must be done in opportunities that can generate high enough returns. If reinvestment is possible only at low returns (below the owner's view of acceptable returns), a business owner is better off withdrawing the cash available for owners from the business instead of allowing the business to reinvest them. Most businesses typically re-invest part of their cash available for owners back into the business in the hopes of growing the business.

I prefer investing in growing enterprises in the Buy-and-Hold Collection. For example, Amazon, Berkshire Hathaway, Tesla, and NU Holdings have been and are continuing to grow. All four generate lots of positive cashflow, but they have been reinvesting a very large portion of their cashflow from operating activities to grow the business.

Lots of businesses can grow but very few large businesses can grow rapidly and profitably while also generating free cashflow and investing enough capital to expand production at a high rate. I search for growing companies that are the exception; I search for companies that are expanding their business, and at the same time, generating free cash flow.

Tesla is an example. Tesla has yet to return cash to shareholders (owners), but Tesla's electric car deliveries have grown rapidly and they have been profitable since 2020. Deliveries have been growing at a greater than 50% compound annual growth rate for the last ten years; that is a high growth rate for such a long duration. After delivering 22,442 vehicles in 2013, Tesla projected a 500,000-delivery target for 2020. The delivery target seemed unreachable, was met by disbelief and even ridicule from legacy automakers and the financial media, but seven years later, Tesla came within 353 vehicles, 0.07%, of its target. In January 2021, Tesla gave further clear guidance: "over a multi-year horizon, we expect to achieve 50% average annual growth in vehicle deliveries." Above is a graph of Tesla's electric vehicle deliveries each year since 2013. You can see they have been growing deliveries at a 55% compound annual growth rate since 2013. The CAGR since 2020 is 54% exceeding the target that was set in 2020 thus far.

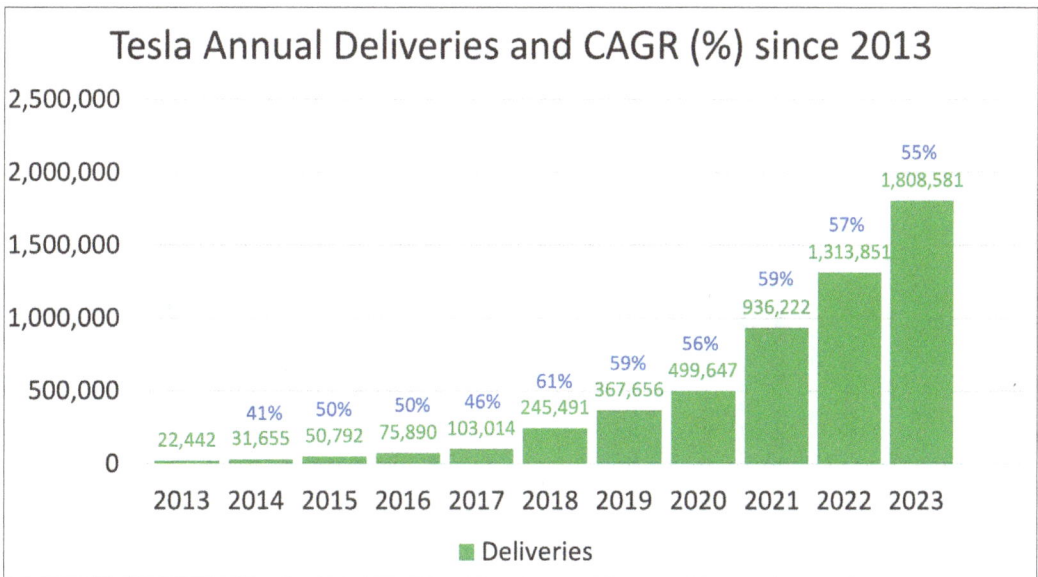

Tesla Annual Deliveries and CAGR (%) since 2013

Year	CAGR	Deliveries
2013		22,442
2014	41%	31,655
2015	50%	50,792
2016	50%	75,890
2017	46%	103,014
2018	61%	245,491
2019	59%	367,656
2020	56%	499,647
2021	59%	936,222
2022	57%	1,313,851
2023	55%	1,808,581

Deliveries

Tesla is aggressively re-investing its cashflow from operating activities (labeled as Operating Cash Flow in the image above) back into the business to allow it to scale volumes and further grow its operations. You can see in the image below that cash flow is positive, but it started to decline after the third quarter of 2022. That cash flow decline is a concern. A big reason for the decline is that, in response to interest rate increases, Tesla began cutting prices for their electric vehicles hoping to maintain their electric vehicle delivery growth. Tesla's cashflow from operating activities still exceeds the amount it is investing to grow the business, creating free cash flow. (Free cash flow is also shown on the same graph above.) The free cash flow being generated was used to pay off all of Tesla's debt and now is quickly creating a large and growing cash pile, over $26 billion as of the third quarter of 2023.

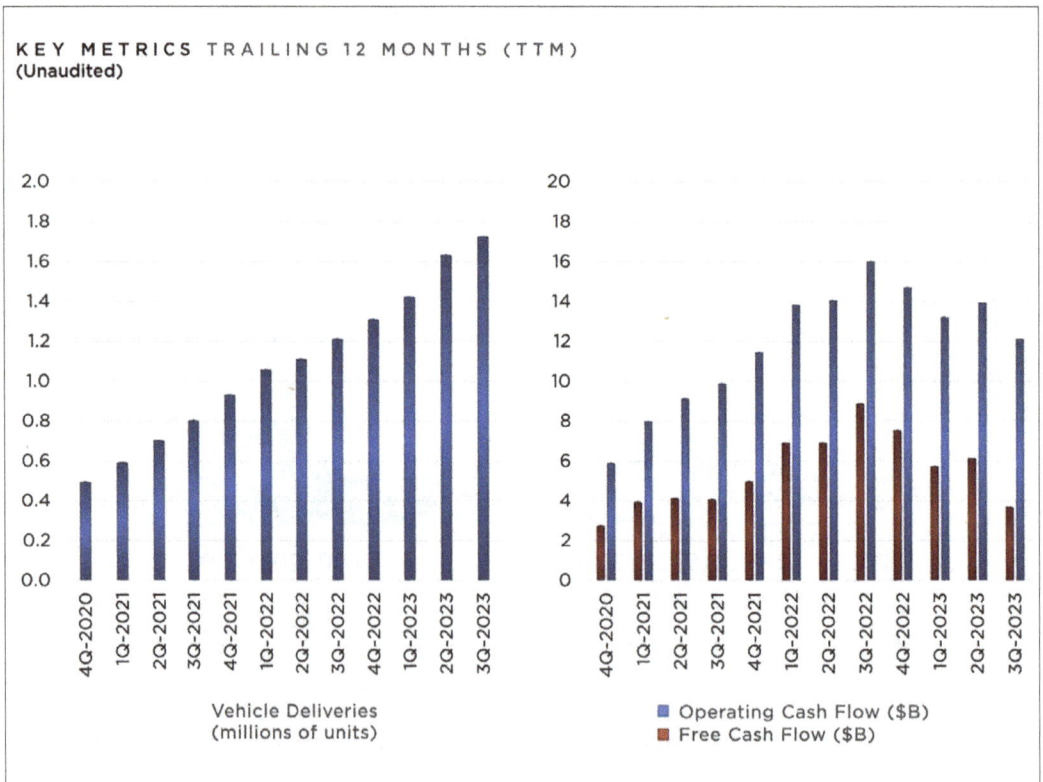

KEY METRICS TRAILING 12 MONTHS (TTM) (Unaudited)

Vehicle Deliveries (millions of units)

Operating Cash Flow ($B)
Free Cash Flow ($B)

Recall that to value a mature business, one with minimal growth, you should imagine the business under normalized conditions; in the case of an oil production company, you had to imagine cash flow from operations and capital intensity with a long-term average oil price and the capital intensity levels necessary to maintain for an extended period the current state of production levels and performance.

When a company, like Tesla, is growing very rapidly and is far away from being mature, your estimates will not be very precise but that is ok if you ensure your decision includes plenty of contingency to reflect the high amount of uncertainty. Remember, you are looking for cinches, not close calls. Unless your analysis concludes that the intrinsic business value could be much more than the stock market's valuation, simply do not purchase the stock. Remind yourself that you do not need to play in everything and move on to something else or wait for conditions to change.

If you wanted to determine Tesla's intrinsic value today, you should imagine what the business will look like once it becomes mature and operating under normalized conditions, or you can imagine how big financially it needs to become to justify a doubling (or more) of the current stock price and estimate how long that would take. In either case, recall the "Law of Large Numbers" from a prior section. Tesla will not be able to keep growing at a 55% CAGR forever. Valuation questions to ponder include:

- What would be a reasonable level of average annual deliveries to assume once the automobile line of business is mature? How long will it be before it reaches that level, and how much will the average profit for each delivery be?

- Tesla has other technology beyond electric cars. What other profitable lines of business exist (energy storage is already profitable and growing) or will exist (supercharger network, software, batteries, solar, robots, artificial intelligence and so on) and how much could those be worth?

The original Tesla shares were purchased in the Buy-and-Hold Collection at the end of 2015 and early in 2016. An intrinsic value estimate of $150 billion in ten years (in 2026) for Tesla seemed possible. It assumed normalized annual cashflow for owners could be more than $5 billion a year by 2026. The analysis assumed Tesla would likely still be growing in 2026, but at a much lower growth rate. Accordingly, the analysis used a 3% real return yield (discount rate) in 2026 instead of the 5% that was used earlier for mature businesses with no growth. A key, and very uncertain, assumption in the analysis at the time was that Tesla could get to at least 2 million car deliveries a year. There was no explicit value assigned to Tesla's non-car businesses (supercharger network, energy storage, and other lines of business), but the analysis assumed additional shares would be issued and the value of the non-vehicle lines of business would offset the per share value dilution that would occur from 2016 through 2026.

When the Tesla shares were bought at the end of 2015 and early in 2016 at an average cost of $15.58 per share, that equated to a $35-billion stock market valuation if you had bought the whole company. If $35 billion grows at a 15% compound annual growth rate, it will increase four times in ten years, resulting in a valuation of $150 billion (35 multiplied by 1.15 ten times). Instead, Tesla's stock price is up 16 times in the eight years since the shares were purchased, a CAGR of 41%. The actual results have turned out better than expected thus far.

NU Holdings is another example of a fast-growing business. NU's smartphone-based digital banking and financial services platform serves 90 million customers using only about 8,000 people in one centralized location (NU has no branch offices), and it does this at a cost to serve that is about 20 times more efficient than traditional banks. (Traditional banks, unlike NU, rely on branch offices.) NU also leverages technology to offer additional products and services to the existing customer base at effectively no incremental customer acquisition cost.

NU's business model generates potent operating leverage as the business scales. Since much of NU's costs are fixed, as the business revenue grows, profits rapidly increase now that revenues are high enough to cover those fixed costs. NU's customer count has been growing, plus they have been earning more from each customer, meaning revenues have been growing faster than customer count. Their cost to serve a customer has been remaining flat. The happy result is that incremental revenue can create net income growth rates that are much higher than the already high revenue growth rates. Refer to the graphs in the image below.

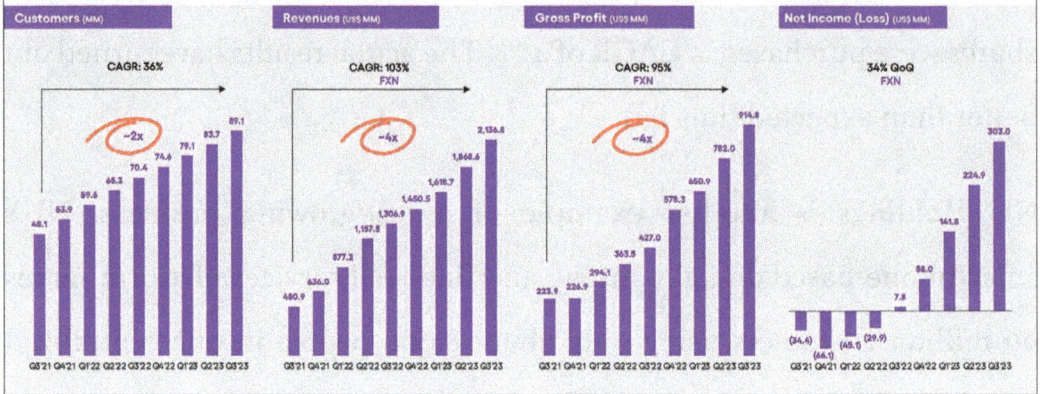

Consistently Compounding Growth, with Meaningful Shift to Profitability

If you wanted to determine NU's intrinsic value today, you can imagine what the business will look like once it becomes mature and operating under normalized conditions. Net Income reached $300 million last quarter, a $1.2 billion annual run rate. Customer count has been growing and is currently at 90 million. NU's average revenue per active customer has also been growing. Can both continue to grow? How large could each become? How large does net income need to become to justify the current stock price as well as double the current stock price? How long would that take?

Whether it is ConocoPhillips, Tesla, NU, or something else, you should write down the date your intrinsic value analysis was done, any key assumptions, any big questions you could not answer, and your estimated intrinsic value. Even when your estimates are very uncertain, still write them down. Make a guess. Write it down. If your initial guess turns out to be incorrect, understand why. Your next guess will likely be a bit better. Over time, you may become quite good at estimating the intrinsic value of businesses.

You want to track business results, not the stock price, and your notes will be valuable for future reference and to monitor progress. The stock price will go up or down in the short term, but all that matters in the long term is the business results—that should be your focus. Over time, you will be surprised to see how disconnected the stock price and the business results can sometimes be.

Ben Graham's approach requires that you have a general understanding of the business and that will eliminate a lot of industries and stocks, especially when you are just beginning. But there are thousands of opportunities in the markets. You do not have to play everywhere. If you know a few spots, your circles of competence, stick to those spots. After all, if you bring nothing to the party, why should you expect to take anything home? Your opportunities may broaden as you gain experience, but you can also stay narrowly focused and still do well.

STOCK ANALYSIS SHOULD BE BUSINESS ANALYSIS

In summary, ownership of stocks is simply a proxy for ownership of the underlying business. So, in turn, stock analysis should be business analysis. If you are interested in purchasing a stock, you should evaluate the business and determine your own independent view of the business's intrinsic value. That intrinsic value may be different from the stock market's view of the business's value. It is in these different views of value where you find ripe opportunities to purchase stocks. This next section will show you how to find the stock market's valuation and how to take advantage of market volatility.

2. VIEW THE MARKET, "MR. MARKET," AS SOMEONE THERE TO SERVE YOU, NOT TO INFORM YOU

In The Intelligent Investor, Ben Graham invented the concept of, "Mr. Market;" it is a very big idea that will help your stock investing. Successful investors in the stock market take to heart the Mr. Market saga, which is vital to having the right attitude toward market fluctuations.

In contrast to your independently derived intrinsic business value, the stock market also provides a value for publicly traded companies, thousands of companies, by continually providing stock price quotes throughout the day.

"In fact, the true investor welcomes volatility. Ben Graham explained why in Chapter 8 of The Intelligent Investor. There he introduced "Mr. Market," an obliging fellow who shows up every day to either buy from you or sell to you, whichever you wish. The more manic-depressive this chap is, the greater the opportunities available to the investor. That's true because a wildly fluctuating market means that irrationally low prices will periodically be attached to solid businesses. It is impossible to see how the availability of such prices can be thought of as increasing the hazards for an investor who is totally free to either ignore the market or exploit its folly."

— WARREN BUFFETT

STOCK MARKET'S VIEW OF BUSINESS VALUE

To determine the stock market's view of the business's value, all you need to know is the current stock price, the total number of shares held by all its shareholders (also called outstanding shares), and the amount of net-debt (debt held by the company minus any cash held by the company). Multiply the total number of shares by the current stock price and that is the stock market's view of the value of the shareholders' portion of the business, often referred to as the stock's "market capitalization" or "equity value." Add the market capitalization to the company's net debt (debtholders' portion of the business) and that would be the market's view of the total value of a publicly traded business, the stock's enterprise value. The market capitalization is how much money it would take, at current stock prices, to buy the whole business while maintaining its existing levels of net-debt. The enterprise value is how much money you would need to purchase all the outstanding shares at the current stock price (shareholders portion) plus the money needed to pay off the net-debt (debtholders' portion).

If you are able and determined to buy the whole business, as you bought out the other shareholders, the stock price will likely rise. Therefore, corporate acquisitions of solid businesses often cost more than current stock prices—buying all the shares of a solid business often requires paying a premium above the current stock price. However, it's important to note that you can buy small pieces of publicly traded businesses, stocks, for less than someone can usually purchase the whole business. If you like bargains, a small investor who can only afford a very small piece of a publicly traded business can access bargains that are not available to a company that is interested in acquiring the whole company.

Let's look at an example of Mr. Market's view of a business's value. On the left side, the image below shows the business analysis of ConocoPhillips which we reviewed earlier, and on the right side, the image shows Mr. Market's view of ConocoPhillips' value back in March of 2020. You can see on the right side of the image that Mr. Market in March of 2020 valued ConocoPhillips market capitalization at about $33 billion (multiply the March 2020 stock price of $31 per share by the total number of shares available, 1.072 billion shares). Therefore, to purchase all of ConocoPhillips' shares from Mr. Market, it would cost about $33 billion in March 2020.

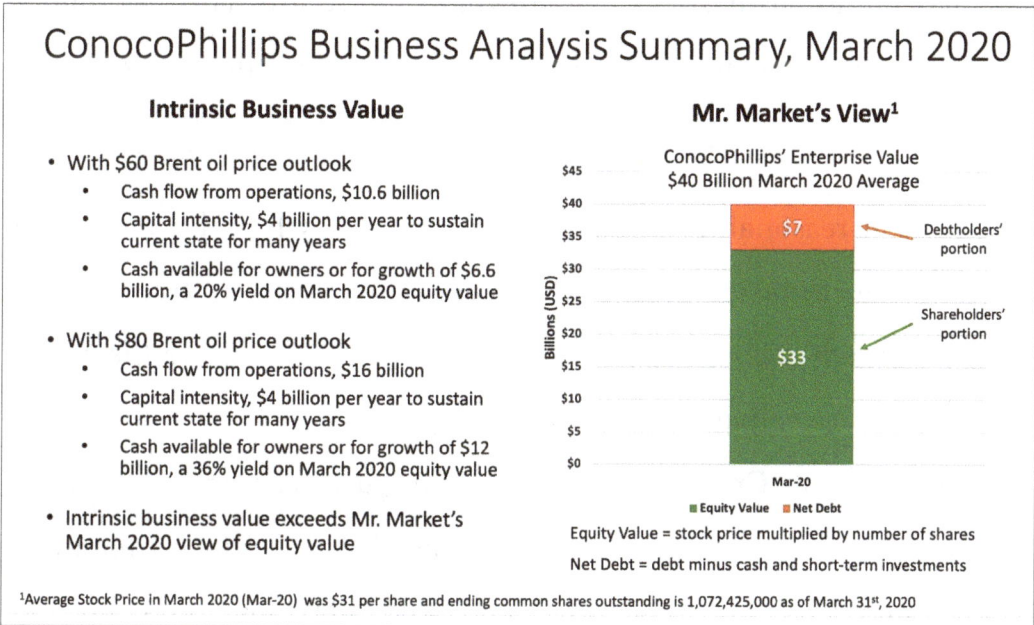

ConocoPhillips Business Analysis Summary, March 2020

Intrinsic Business Value

- With $60 Brent oil price outlook
  - Cash flow from operations, $10.6 billion
  - Capital intensity, $4 billion per year to sustain current state for many years
  - Cash available for owners or for growth of $6.6 billion, a 20% yield on March 2020 equity value

- With $80 Brent oil price outlook
  - Cash flow from operations, $16 billion
  - Capital intensity, $4 billion per year to sustain current state for many years
  - Cash available for owners or for growth of $12 billion, a 36% yield on March 2020 equity value

- Intrinsic business value exceeds Mr. Market's March 2020 view of equity value

Mr. Market's View[1]

ConocoPhillips' Enterprise Value
$40 Billion March 2020 Average

$7 — Debtholders' portion

$33 — Shareholders' portion

Billions (USD): $0, $5, $10, $15, $20, $25, $30, $35, $40, $45

Mar-20

■ Equity Value ■ Net Debt

Equity Value = stock price multiplied by number of shares

Net Debt = debt minus cash and short-term investments

[1]Average Stock Price in March 2020 (Mar-20) was $31 per share and ending common shares outstanding is 1,072,425,000 as of March 31st, 2020

Based on the March 2020 business analysis, real returns on the purchase price would have averaged about 20% per year if oil prices averaged the more modest $60 per Brent barrel ($6.6 billion of annual cash divided by a $33 billion investment to purchase all the shares) or 36% per year if oil prices averaged $80 per Brent barrel ($12 billion divided by $33 billion). A 20% real return outlook in March of 2020 was silly cheap, very attractive. Recall that the stock market's overall average nominal return has been about 10% compounded annually over the long term, equivalent to a 7% real return (when adjusted for inflation).

Recall from the earlier section, based on the model and discounted cashflow analysis, if you could purchase all of ConocoPhillips for $100 billion at the beginning of 2020, you could expect to earn about a 10%

nominal and 7% real annual return with a $60 real Brent average oil price forecast and no business volume growth in the future. The $100 billion intrinsic value estimate was triple the stock's market value of $33 billion in March 2020.

Therefore, a reasonable estimate (no volume growth and a modest oil price) of the intrinsic value of ConocoPhillips' business exceeded Mr. Market's March 2020 stock price value by 200%, three times the March 2020 stock price valuation, providing a huge margin of safety for a stock purchase decision. Crucially, if a shareholder purchases only a small part interest (a few shares of the total shares) instead of the entire company, the small shareholder's return on investment would have been the same: your stock purchase in March 2020 would be worth triple what you would have paid in the stock market, a bargain, and your outlook for average overall returns over the long-term would be a greater than 20% real annual return.

Mr. Market's view of value will sometimes be much different than your estimate of intrinsic business value. The stock price at times can become totally disconnected from the underlying business results. You want to buy from Mr. Market when he is pessimistic about the stock of interest. ConocoPhillips' production was not growing from 2016 through 2019, but their improvements in operating cash flow and capital intensity were impressive and beneficial to shareholders plus the company wisely used its free cashflow to reduce debt levels and repurchase shares during the same period. Those actions were sound and grew ConocoPhillips' intrinsic business value per share, but Mr. Market did not seem to notice. Mr. Market was pessimistic about ConocoPhillips's value in March of 2020.

However, by the end of 2022, Mr. Market's mood had changed dramatically, he was much more optimistic about ConocoPhillips and valued the business at a market capitalization of $144 billion: the stock price had increased rapidly, was valued at $118 per share, and the total number of shares was 1,223,856,000. Refer to the stock price chart below.

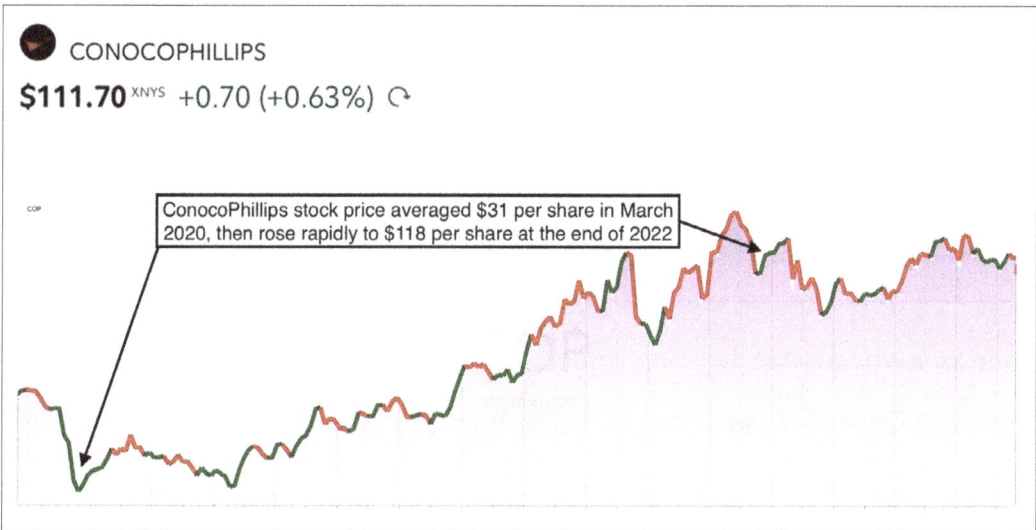

CONOCOPHILLIPS

$111.70 XNYS +0.70 (+0.63%)

ConocoPhillips stock price averaged $31 per share in March 2020, then rose rapidly to $118 per share at the end of 2022

Mr. Market's view of ConocoPhillips' market capitalization (shareholders' portion) increased more than four times in less than 3 years from a market capitalization of $33 to 144 billion: the growth in market capitalization was a 71% CAGR from March 2020 through December 2022. ConocoPhillips' stock price in the same period went from $31 per share to $118 per shares, a 63% CAGR, slightly less since the share count expanded but still an exceptional return for shareholders.

ConocoPhillips compound annual growth rate = $(144/33)^{\wedge}(1/2.75) - 1 = 71\%$

The intrinsic value of a large, mature business such as ConocoPhillips would typically only change gradually; you would not derive a four times intrinsic value change in such a short timeframe. In fact, the intrinsic value of the business had not drastically changed, but Mr. Market's mood had changed. The stock price of $31 per share in 2020 was very undervalued compared to the intrinsic value of the business.

> *"The beauty of stocks is they... sell at silly prices from time to time.*
> *That's how Charlie and I have gotten rich. ... Ben Graham writes*
> *about it in Chapter 8 of the Intelligent Investor."*
> — WARREN BUFFETT

You, as a successful investor, need to decouple your assessment of the business from its jiggling stock price because you want to discover those times when the stock price is no longer linked with the results of the underlying business.

ConocoPhillips is a mature business with limited growth potential. Let's now look at a couple of growth companies to further illustrate how Mr. Market can be irrational at times.

When Amazon shares were purchased on September 9, 1997, twenty-six years ago, Mr. Market was willing to sell you all of Amazon's shares for only about $1.5 billion. I was living in London back then, home to some of the world's best bookstores, but I preferred Amazon's buying experience. The business had a clear vision, a much more efficient business model, and a focus on business execution. Internet commerce was still new, with lots of uncertainty, but it seemed obvious—no discounted cashflow analysis was required. The business was worth much more than Mr. Market's price of $1.5 billion back in 1997.

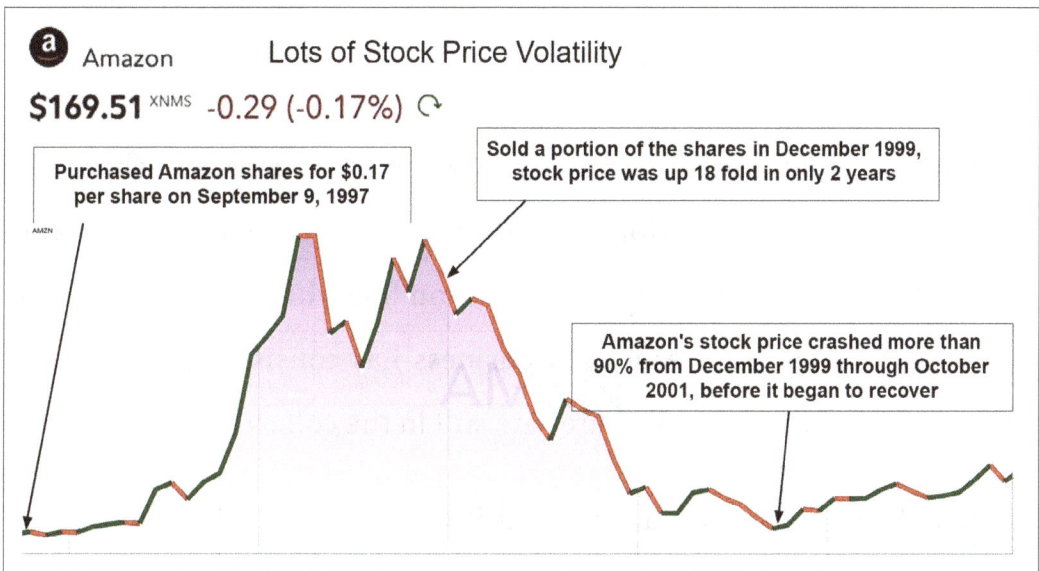

A couple of years later, at the end of 1999, Mr. Market had changed its tune and now loved Amazon and almost anything else that could be considered an "internet" stock, even though many internet companies at the time were terrible businesses. Mr. Market didn't care about business fundamentals though; he wasn't able to distinguish between a poor business and Amazon's business. Mr. Market was swept up in "irrational exuberance," a phrase coined by the Federal Reserve Board Chairman, Alan Greenspan, when describing the dot-com bubble of the late 1990s. He used the term to warn investors that many stocks were likely to be overvalued.

After the initial purchase of Amazon shares, the stock price took off very quickly. A portion of the shares were sold in December 1999, about two years after the initial purchase. The stock was up 18 times the initial purchase price in only two years, equating to a 324% compound annual growth rate for the two-year period, an unbelievable return.

$$\text{Amazon CAGR for first 2 years} = (18)^{\wedge}(1/2) - 1 = 324\% \text{ CAGR}$$

It is so rare to find a good business that, when it happens, you should be reluctant to sell the stock as long as the business continues to perform well. Ignore the stock price movements while you hold the stock of a business that is performing well. Amazon's business has consistently performed well, so some of the original shares are still in the collection to this day.

Holding Amazon turned out well, but it was a very volatile ride. After a portion of the original Amazon shares were sold, the stock price fell more than 90% from December of 1999 through October of 2001, even though the business was performing at a high level throughout the period. The greater than 90% drop was emotionally difficult to ignore at the time.

"Everyone has the brainpower to make money in stocks.
Not everyone has the stomach."
— PETER LYNCH

Here is another example, like ConocoPhillips in 2020 and Amazon in 2000, of how irrational and disconnected from the underlying business fundamentals Mr. Market can be. The buy-and-hold collection purchased $10,020 worth of stock in Cisco Systems in September 1996. Cisco, like Amazon, was another growth stock in the internet space. Cisco was a good company, but its stock price, soon after it was purchased, was swept upwards by irrational exuberance. Cisco's stock price rose more than 21 times the purchase price by early 2000, from $3.71 to $80 per share in less than 4 years.

Cisco's rise was even more puzzling than Amazon's because Cisco's good business performance was nothing close to what could justify such an elevated stock price. The market capitalization was approaching $500 billion, and that was more than twenty-three years ago when it was a lot of money. I became more worried when management began ignoring, or forgetting, sound business principles to justify Mr. Market's valuation. An example was Cisco began advocating that employee stock compensation should not be viewed as a business cost. Compensation is a business cost, and the cost of the employee stock compensation program wasn't theoretical, it was obvious. At that time, Cisco was spending large amounts of cash to repurchase shares at irrationally exuberant stock prices (a poor use of cash, destroying value) to partially offset the share count dilution being created by their lucrative employee stock compensation.

I sold about a third of the stock on March 27, 2000, at $80.25 per share, and sold the remaining shares soon after. The average price sold for all the shares was at $67 per share, up 18 times the purchase price in only 4 years, a 106% compound annual growth rate (returns more than doubled each year for four years).

Today, more than 23 years later, Cisco's stock price has still not recovered to the prices seen back in 2000. Being patient is important, but 23 years is a long time. Cisco's stock closed this year at $50.52 per share. Reference the stock chart graph below.

Bought $10,020 of Cisco stock, $3.71 per share on September 3, 1996

CISCO SYSTEMS INC
$50.09 XNMS +0.01 (+0.

Sold $181,380 of Cisco stock, starting March 2000 and completed by October, at an average price of $67 per share, one-thirds at $80, 65 and 55 per share

Importantly, if I had kept the original Cisco shares in the collection, the gain over 27 years would have been below my 15% CAGR target, but surprisingly, it would still have been better than the average investor. If the Cisco shares were kept, the investment would have been up almost 14 times the 1996 purchase price, or a 10% compound annual growth rate for 27 years. That return is much less than what was achieved in only 4 years by making the decision back in 2000 to sell the Cisco shares to an irrationally exuberant Mr. Market.

The Cisco experience also highlights something else that will be fundamental to your investment success: Your purchase price is important. If Cisco shares were kept, it would have worked out ok only because the shares were bought early, before the bubble inflated the stock price to irrational levels. Someone who bought Cisco later, near its highs, instead of having a profit would have lost money.

Too many people look to the stock market to inform them. Academia has not been helpful in this regard. "Efficient Market Theory" was very popular, taught at universities and believed by many people. The hypothesis is that share prices reflect all information, and stocks always trade at their fair value on public exchanges, making it impossible for investors to purchase undervalued stocks or sell stocks at inflated prices. Therefore, the efficient market hypothesis would imply that it is impossible to outperform the overall market through stock selection, suggesting that investors would do better by investing in a low-cost, passive portfolio (like an index fund). Not surprisingly, some providers of index funds continue to be proponents of Efficient Market Theory: "whose bread I eat, his song I sing."

I was enrolled at Massachusetts Institute of Technology (MIT), in Cambridge, Massachusetts, earning a master's degree, when I decided to sell my Cisco shares in 2000. Efficient Market Theory had a few proponents even there, but I was not one of them. I have many, many examples, and not just with ConocoPhillips, Amazon, and Cisco, that give me confidence that efficient market theory is complete bunk in the short term.

> *"The market is a pendulum that forever swings between unsustainable optimism (which makes stocks too expensive) and unjustified pessimism (which makes them too cheap). The intelligent investor is a realist who sells to optimists and buys from pessimists."*
> — BEN GRAHAM

To be clear, the market is aligned with the business in the long term. If a business does well or poorly, the stock eventually follows, but it may take the stock a very long time and, in some cases, years. Ben Graham describes the difference this way:

> *"In the short run, the market is like a voting machine —*
> *tallying up which firms are popular and unpopular.*
> *But in the long run, the market is like a weighing machine —*
> *assessing the substance of a company."*
> — BEN GRAHAM

You do not know how the stock market will perform tomorrow, or next month, or even next year. What you can and should do is build a heavier and heavier portfolio. Try to select stocks of good to wonderful businesses, companies that want to be weighed. Over time, they will be. Over the long term, all companies are. Know that if you own stocks in good businesses and the businesses continue to execute well, the odds for a positive outcome in the stock market tilt ever more in your favor the longer you hold. So that is what you focus on.

If the business continues to perform well, try to ignore the stock price movements and the chatter, spin, and general nonsense from secondary sources (brokers, stock analysts, business news media, and more). Focus on company disclosures instead — earnings calls, investor presentations, financials, and so on.

Buy good businesses, don't overpay, and hold them as long as they remain good businesses; it just seems too easy, but creating wealth by investing in stocks is difficult for people to do. Successful stock investing does not require a great amount of intelligence. An ability to detach yourself from the crowd, to tune out the market noise, is the quality a successful investor needs most.

> *"Nobody else has my view. It doesn't bother me.*
> *I just think they're all wrong."*
> — CHARLIE MUNGER

If the business continues to perform well, continue to hold your shares. Compare actual business performance to your own estimates. Update your business analysis notes over time as the business progresses. If the business performance starts to degrade, consider selling your shares if Mr. Market offers up an attractive price relative to your independently derived view of business value.

> *"We derive no comfort because important people, vocal people, or great numbers of people agree with us. Nor do we derive comfort if they don't. A public opinion poll is no substitute for thought. When we really sit back with a smile on our face is when we run into a situation we can understand, where the facts are ascertainable and clear, and the course of action is obvious. In that case – whether conventional or unconventional – whether others agree or disagree – we feel we are progressing in a conservative manner."*
> — WARREN BUFFETT, PARTNERSHIP LETTER

Also try to ignore the macroeconomic environment when making investment decisions. At the very least, resist the temptation to change your investment stance because of something you think might happen in the headlines. You would have to be right about the macro event and have to foresee the correct consequences in the real world to know the correct consequences on stock prices. Getting all this right is very rare. Peter Lynch likes to say, "If as a stock investor you spend 14 minutes every year focused on macroeconomics, you wasted 12 minutes. I really believe that." Instead, focus on how well the business is performing.

Sometimes you will find a terrific business but will have to wait a very long time, years, before Mr. Market offers it at a price attractive enough for you to purchase the stock. Learn to enjoy the waiting part of investing. Maintain your estimate of intrinsic value, updating it based on business results over time. You may not be very outwardly active, based on trading frequency, but you will be ready to act should Mr. Market's mood tilt in your desired direction.

> *"The market quotes you prices every day; you can take it or leave it and there are no called strikes. You will have periods with significant levels of inactivity if you swing at only the best pitches. Inactivity is sometimes undervalued. Important to distinguish when you are in a situation where your number of swings are limited but you have no called strikes."*
> — WARREN BUFFETT

Ben Graham's view of Mr. Market is a more useful and lucrative concept than Efficient Market Theory: Mr. Market is not some sort of divine oracle; he is a manic depressive. You shouldn't be informed by him, but he can serve you. He can be useful to a rational investor who decides to buy from Mr. Market when irrationally low prices are attached to solid businesses and sell to Mr. Market when irrationally high prices exist.

Question: *"You said before most of what investors see are false phenomena. How should we think about that? Where is the truth then? How can we get to the truth?"*

Charlie Munger: *"A lot of people think there is such a thing as the truth in the market and that the market tells you something just by bouncing around. That is not the way Berkshire Hathaway or Charlie Munger invests money. We have a view as to what the intrinsic value is and what is being traded. And we only buy it when we think it's worth more than we are paying. So we are trying to make a long-term investment by waiting for something to be underpriced and then buying it. And we don't give a damn about all those gamblers in the market. To me, they are so much froth. It's a foolish way to spend your time if you want to get rich that way. We've put a lot of money to work during the chaos of the last two years. It's been an ideal period for investors: A climate of fear is their best friend. Those who invest only when commentators are upbeat end up paying a heavy price for meaningless reassurance. In the end, what counts in investing is what you pay for a business—through the purchase of a small piece of it in the stock market—and what the business earns in the succeeding decade or two."*

And finally, the third cornerstone idea for selecting stocks is to ensure you have a margin of safety.

3. ENSURE YOU HAVE A MARGIN OF SAFETY.

A final and essential step in Ben Graham's approach to investing is the "margin of safety." No matter how careful you are, there are always risks. Ben Graham's approach insists that, if you decide to buy a stock, the stock price should be below, cheaper than, your own independently derived estimate of the business's intrinsic value. The difference between Mr. Market's price and your own estimate is the margin of safety. If you have a good understanding of a business and the future of the business, you will need little in the way of margin of safety. The more uncertainty, assuming you still want to invest in it, the larger the margin of safety you would need.

You should be cautious with future investments—you may not succeed. Warren teaches that you will improve your financial well-being if you imagine you have a 20-slot punch card. Each punch represents the investments you will make over your lifetime, and after you punched through the card, you are not allowed to make any more investments. Under those rules, you would be more selective and committed about the investments you decide to make. You would be forced to trim away lots of mediocre ideas and would commit material amounts to only your best opportunities. If you pour your limited resources (time, effort, and savings) into only 20 great ideas over an investment lifetime, and out of those 20 only a few may work out, it will be much more financially rewarding than trying a new idea every day.

Now for me, because my natural inclination is to be an optimist, I often recall Housman's poem in an attempt to maintain rationality when making investment decisions:

> *The thoughts of others*
> *Were light and fleeting,*
> *Of lovers' meeting*
> *Or luck or fame.*
> *Mine were of trouble,*

And mine were steady,

So I was ready

When trouble came.

— Alfred Edward Housman

The world is uncertain. Life's rich pattern consists of ups as well as downs. Many surprises will be unpleasant. Life can hit you. And when it does, it often hits hard. But rather than wallow in our struggles—whether financially related or otherwise—you need to find a way to move forward. Go through life anticipating trouble and be ready to perform adequately if trouble comes.

After paying $12,609.85 for my first Berkshire Hathaway share in 1993, I tracked Berkshire Hathaway's business performance on a regular basis, and I tried to only look at Mr. Market's value on a periodic basis. It took five years before I bought more shares of Berkshire Hathaway. Then I bought more shares six times from 1998 through 2021 and never sold any Berkshire Hathaway shares prior to 2022.

That is only seven short spurts of buying activity over twenty-nine years. Each time, what I paid (Mr. Market's value) has been lower than my own independently derived intrinsic value for Berkshire Hathaway. There were a few more times during that period when I noticed Mr. Market's valuation was underpriced, but I did not always have funds available to purchase shares, or I was too slow to act before the stock price rose beyond the target purchase price. My low trading frequency with Berkshire stock resulted in low fees, and by not selling any Berkshire stock, I deferred paying capital gains taxes on 29 years of unrealized gains.

As covered in a prior section, the first share of Berkshire Hathaway has returned 13% compounded annually over 30 years. Each additional share was purchased with a margin of safety, and that improved my overall Berkshire Hathaway returns above 13% compounded annually—much better than the overall market's average compound annual growth rate of 10%. Recall that even small differences in compound annual growth rates over 30 years will result in very large differences in wealth thanks to the higher returns and the magic of compounding over long periods. I have several investments that have generated better returns, but none of them have been more useful to me than Berkshire Hathaway. I learn best by doing. It was my investment in Berkshire Hathaway and Warren Buffett's advice over the years that helped me understand Ben Graham's ideas and how to apply them. I make investing mistakes, plenty of mistakes, but I have been able to apply the same methodology to other stocks with good results overall.

"If you look to 'Mr. Market' for advice, you are destined to fail.
But if you look to Mr. Market for opportunity,
if you attempt to take advantage of the emotional extremes,
then you are very likely to succeed over time."
— BEN GRAHAM

Berkshire Hathaway and many of the other stocks in the buy-and-hold collection do not pay dividends. I am not against buying dividend paying stocks, and I own some. My investing focus is on finding good to wonderful businesses that I can buy for a reasonable price. Dividends are just not my focus.

For those of you who want stock dividends, Warren has been actively demonstrating for many years how a shareholder can effectively generate their own dividend-type income by selling shares. The concept was first introduced by Franco Modigliani, an economics Nobel Prize winner. I had the pleasure of meeting Mr. Modigliani, many years ago, and found him inspiring. Mr. Modigliani passed away in 2003.

Every year since June 26, 2006, Warren donates 4% of his Berkshire shares to charities. When his schedule for annual charitable grants started, 17 years ago, Warren owned 474,998 Berkshire shares, worth about $44 billion based on the stock price at the start (the stock price was $92,000 per share).

Berkshire Hathaway has been successful and is now one of the largest businesses in the world, with almost 400,000 employees, but Warren's Berkshire compensation has been modest, at only a $100,000 annual salary since the grants started; furthermore, Warren received no salary increases, no bonuses, no stock options, nor had any stock grants added to his compensation from Berkshire. Warren has also not bought or sold any shares in Berkshire Hathaway during the period.

After giving away 256,711 shares, 54% of his starting share count, his remaining shares (218,287 shares) were worth about $120 billion at the end of 2023 (the stock price was $543,000 per share).

Warren is much wealthier now than he was when he started donating 4% to charity 17 years ago—just another excellent example of the magic and power of compounding over long periods of time.

Berkshire Hathaway does not pay a dividend, but Warren's approach results in the same outcome as if he had received a 4% annual dividend. Importantly, Warren's approach also removes two disadvantages of dividends: 1.) different investors may desire different levels of payouts, and 2.) a dividend received is taxed as income, which long-term investors may not want.

You can use the same concept as Warren to generate income with your own retirement buy-and-hold portfolio if the dividend payout is lower than what you want.

If Warren had kept all his shares, they would be worth $260 billion using the year-end 2023 share price of $543,000 per share ($543,000 multiplied by 474,998). Warren's current ownership consists of 218,287 shares and those shares are worth about $120 billion (543,000 multiplied by 218,287).

The story also illustrates another, of many, positive impacts Warren Buffett is making in the world.

SUCCESSFUL INVESTORS BECOME LEARNING MACHINES

Returning to the video that I recommended at the beginning of this section, when Warren references a friend who says, "To a man with a hammer, everything looks like a nail." The friend he is talking about is Charlie Munger.

> *"It is kind of fun to sit there and out-think people who are way smarter than you are because you've trained yourself to be more objective and more multidisciplinary. Furthermore, there is a lot of money in it, as I can testify from my own personal experience."*
> — CHARLIE MUNGER

Charlie was a 99-year-old polymath. He was a World War II veteran, Harvard law school graduate, a founding partner of the elite Munger, Tolles, and Olson law firm, owner of an investment firm that significantly outperformed the market, Chairman of Wesco Financial Corporation, Vice Chairman of Berkshire Hathaway, CEO and Chairman of Daily Journal Corporation, Costco director, and well-read and self-taught in many diverse subjects.

> *"An investment in knowledge pays the best interest."*
> — BENJAMIN FRANKLIN

As usual, Charlie is right. You really do not want to be someone who only has a hammer. Instead, you should learn the big ideas in the big disciplines and use them regularly, expanding your toolkit to more than just a hammer.

Life is full of uncertainties, but one certain thing is the world is full of wonders. Explore them. Be a lifelong learner. Nearly everything is interesting if you go into it deeply enough. You should encourage your curiosity; be interested in ideas, collect, and use the best of them, often. Think for yourself. Don't care about what others think of you. Embrace uncertainty, humility, and humor. Don't be afraid to ask questions. If you keep learning all the time, you will have a wonderful advantage in life, and you will not be disappointed.

> *"Have the courage of your knowledge and experience. If you have formed a conclusion from the facts and if you know your judgment is sound, act on it — even though others may hesitate or differ. (You are neither right nor wrong because the crowd disagrees with you. You are right because your data and reasoning are right.) Similarly, in the world of securities, courage becomes the supreme virtue after adequate knowledge and a tested judgment are at hand."*
> — BEN GRAHAM

The world gives you clues, and an investor is like a detective who has an endless series of mysteries to try and solve. This is precisely the task of an intelligent investor. Investors take the accumulated worldly wisdom they have obtained in life and apply that to the analysis of businesses within their individual circles of competence, and then they make judgments regarding the relative attractiveness of businesses.

WRAP UP: HOW TO CHOOSE THE RIGHT STOCKS

A summary and suggestions:

- It will be the quality of the underlying business that you invest in which determines your returns when shares of stock are held for decades because, over the long term, it's unlikely for a stock to earn a much better return than the business which underlies it.
  - Buy good to wonderful businesses.
  - Once purchased, you should then hold the stocks for as long as they remain good businesses.
  - Your goal should be to find underlying businesses that you can own for many decades and that can become compounding machines.

- The most effective way to select stocks for long-term investments is to utilize Ben Graham's big three ideas, repeated below:
  - Stocks are just pieces of businesses. You purchase small pieces, part interest, of businesses that happen to be publicly traded in the stock markets (stocks).
  - View the market, "Mr. Market," as someone there to serve you, not to inform you.

- Ensure you have a Margin of Safety. If you decide to buy a stock, the stock price should be below your own independently derived estimate of the business's value.

- A key to investing is learning how to determine your own independently derived value estimate, also known as the intrinsic value, for the business.
    - To be clear, the intrinsic value is not dependent on the stock price.
    - Once derived, the intrinsic value may be close to the stock market's view of value, but it also may be different.

- What you hope to find are intrinsic values that exceed the market's view of value because that provides you with an opportunity to buy the shares of stock in the stock market for less than what you believe the underlying business is worth.
    - Your intrinsic value estimate does not need to be precise. Reasonable minds will differ. You are looking for cinches, not close calls. A roughly right estimate will do. Businesses accrue value over years.
    - Mr. Market's view of value (stock price), on the other hand, is available daily, and even more frequently than that, and sometimes it changes drastically in a short period of time.

- Start by imagining you are buying the whole business, under normalized conditions, and you will then compare your independently derived value estimate to Mr. Market's view of value.

- What matters for business value is understanding the business's cash flow. The amount of cash the business can return to its owners over time, from now through the future.

- You can use the 'Business as a Box' mental model to imagine what it would take for the business of interest to be equivalent to a box that can spit out cash for its owner (or owners) year after year, for many years, with no degradation over time in the business's cash-creation capability.

- Capital intensity is how much cash a company needs to spend each year on average to sustain (with no growth and no decline) their current state for many years. It is not an accounting term, but it is all important and you can discover it if you know to look for it.

- The difference between cashflow from operating activities and capital intensity will be the cash available for owners after sustaining the current state, or if retained by the business and not paid out to owners, it could be used to grow the business.

- Write down the date you did the analysis, your key assumptions, outstanding questions, and your intrinsic value estimate for future reference and to monitor progress.

- When a company is growing very rapidly and is far away from being mature, your intrinsic value estimates will not be very precise but that is okay if you ensure your decision includes plenty of contingency to compensate for the high amount of uncertainty.

- High-quality, growing businesses can grow and still generate free cash flow. Search for companies that are expanding their business, and at the same time, generating free cash flow.

o Free cash flow is cash flow from operations minus capital investments. The free cash flow level for a no growth and no decline scenario would be equal to the normalized cash available for owners estimate that is derived from the Business as a Box methodology. The free cash flow level for a growth scenario will be lower than for a no growth scenario but free cash flow can still be positive if it is a high-quality growing business.

o When you see a growing business, one of the things to look at is the number of shares and the debt levels over an extended period. If the share count and debt levels are stable or declining, but not increasing, and the business is growing, that is likely to be a high-quality growing business.

o Companies that raise debt or issue additional shares to expand their business can sometimes be justified but the existing owners' (shareholders) portion of the business gets diluted and that may not be a good thing for existing owners (you).

o For rapidly growing businesses you can also imagine how big (valuable) it needs to become to justify double the current stock price and assess how long it will take.

- Unless your analysis concludes that the intrinsic business value could be much more than the stock market's valuation, simply do not purchase the stock. Move on to something else or wait for conditions to change.

- The stock market's, Mr. Market's, view of business value, is readily available. Here is what you need to know to determine the stock market's view of value:
  - Current stock price,
  - Total number of shares available,
  - Amount of net-debt (debt held by the company minus any cash held by the company).
  - Multiply the number of shares by the current stock price and that is the stock market's view of the value of the shareholders' portion of the business, often referred to as the stock's "market capitalization" or "equity value."
  - Add the market capitalization to the company's net debt (debt holders' portion of the business) and that would be the market's view of the total value of a publicly traded business, the stock's enterprise value.
  - The market capitalization is also how much money it would take, at current stock prices, to buy the whole business while maintaining its existing levels of net-debt.

- To successfully invest it is vital that you have right attitude toward stock market fluctuations.
  - View the short-term market, Mr. Market, as someone there to serve you, not to inform you. Mr. Market should not be viewed as some sort of divine oracle; he is a manic depressive. You should not be

informed by Mr. Market, but he can serve you; he can be useful to a rational investor who decides to buy from Mr. Market when irrationally low prices are attached to solid businesses and to sell to Mr. Market when irrationally high stock prices exist.

- You need to decouple your assessment of a business from its stock performance, many days and for extended periods the two do not go together.

- To be clear, the market is aligned with the business in the long term. If a business does well or poorly, the stock price eventually follows, but it may take the stock a very, very long time. A business and its stock can become detached from each other for years.

- If you can buy a good business from Mr. Market at a cheaper price than your independently derived value estimate, buy shares and keep the shares as long they remain good businesses.

  - Recall Ben Graham's view that although the market is a voting machine in the short run, in the long run, the market is like a weighing machine, assessing the substance of a company.

  - Build a heavier and heavier portfolio. Try to select companies that want to be weighed. Over time, they will be weighed. Over the long term all companies are.

- The difference between Mr. Market's price for the business and your own estimate of intrinsic value is the margin of safety. The more uncertainty, assuming you still want to invest in it, the larger the margin of safety you would need. You should be cautious with future investments—you may not succeed.

- It is rare to find a good business at an attractive stock price, so be reluctant to sell stock that you have purchased. Focus on monitoring the business performance, set a few targets (cashflow, margins, capital intensity, volumes, or something else—it will depend on the business), monitor against those targets, listen to its management, review business results, and so on.

- Just accept that you will not, and cannot, know how the market will perform tomorrow, or next month, or even next year. Know that if you own stocks in good businesses and the businesses continue to execute well, the odds for a positive outcome in the stock market tilt ever more in your favor the longer you hold. So that is what you focus on.

- If the business continues to perform well, try to ignore the stock price movements and the chatter, spin, and general nonsense from secondary sources (brokers, stock analysts, and business news media). Focus on company disclosures.

- Try to ignore the macroeconomic environment when making investment decisions. At the very least, resist the temptation to change your investment stance because of something you think might happen in the headlines. You would have to be right about the macro event. You would have to foresee the correct consequences in the real world.

You would have to foresee the correct consequences in stock prices. Getting all this right is pretty rare. Peter Lynch likes to say, "If as a stock investor you spend 12 minutes every year focused on macroeconomics, you wasted 12 minutes. I really believe that." Instead focus on how well the business is performing.

- Ben Graham's approach requires that you have a general understanding of the business and that will eliminate a lot of industries and stocks. There are thousands of opportunities in the markets. You do not have to play everywhere. If you know a few spots, your circles of competence, stick to those spots.

- You should learn the big ideas in the big disciplines and use them regularly. If you keep learning all the time, you will have a wonderful advantage in life.

I could discuss investing in publicly traded stocks in more detail, and there are lots of topics that I have not covered, but for the sake of keeping this condensed, I've focused on the need-to-knows, spending less time on the nice-to-knows. But I can always provide more information if there is interest.

Now, let's cover another way to create wealth: selling options!

SELLING
STOCK OPTIONS

I have been a buy-and-hold investor for 30 years, buying shares in good to wonderful businesses at a reasonable price and holding them for as long as they remain good businesses. The goal is building long-term capital appreciation at a rate greater than 15% CAGR. I plan to continue to be a buy-and-hold investor, but what has changed is that, since April 2022, I now also use a portion of my investment portfolio to sell call and put stock option contracts. I am pleased with the outcomes, and I already know I will continue to sell options with a portion of my portfolio.

The reason to bother with selling options at all is because it can be lucrative. Selling options can generate income from assets (stocks or cash) that you already own by collecting premiums each time you sell to open an option contract. Selling options can also allow you to sell shares that you already own at a higher than current market price, and it can allow you to purchase stock at a lower than current market price.

People struggle to learn new skills for many reasons, but one reason is they too quickly get discouraged. Selling options will seem difficult at first, but most things seem difficult at first. To get good at something new, you must be willing to be bad at it. The ability to sit with discomfort through that period of being bad is a very underrated ability; if you are new to selling options, view selling options as an opportunity to develop your capacity to sit with the discomfort of being bad while you learn. Developing that capacity can become a superpower that will be beneficial in many areas of, and throughout, your life.

Stock option trading can be complicated and risky. I have been curious about trading options for almost thirty years but decided back then that I was too busy with my career to start, and I put it on the list of things to do when I retire. I participated in multiple training courses and researched the topic extensively before beginning to sell options in April 2022. I wish I had started sooner, but with all the preparations I made, I was ready, eager, and gained experience quickly.

I experimented with lots of stock option strategies. The approach defined and settled on is simple, does not take much time, has low risks, and is lucrative. Recall that my target is to achieve more than a 20% compound annual growth rate for the selling options portfolio. My actual results for all option trades are an overall 30% CAGR thus far, exceeding my target by a large margin. The 30% CAGR result is all inclusive, which includes many mistakes and trades that were made with several different strategies. It has been 639 days (from April 2022 through year-end 2023) since I began selling options, less than two years, and I will continue to track my results.

The selling options strategy I developed is different from most option strategies. I am willing to learn from others, but frankly, I have been disappointed, and even disagreed, with much of the third-party learning resources that I have found. My dissatisfaction with third-party resources is one of the reasons I wrote *Wealthy & Wise*. Plus, explaining something new and complicated to others is an effective and fun way for me to ensure I understand it.

> *"If you want to master something, teach it."*
> — RICHARD FEYNMAN

Let's introduce, or review, some basics before covering the selling options strategy.

STOCK OPTIONS

You may not be familiar with stock options, but many other types of options have been commonplace for centuries. For example, insurance is a type of option contract. An insurance company sells a contract, valid for a defined duration, that obligates the insurance company to protect the value of a home, car, or whatever, should its value fall. The buyer of the insurance contract pays a premium to the seller. The amount of premium is dependent on the asset being insured, the duration of the contract, the probability of the value threshold being breached during the contract duration, and other factors. When an insurance contract expires, the insurance buyer will often buy a new insurance contract and the insurance seller will collect more premiums.

Now, let's compare insurance options to stock options. You can buy or sell two types of stock option contracts: Calls and Puts. Call stock options give the right to buy a stock and Put stock options give the right to sell a stock at a pre-determined price (the "strike price"), at any time on or before the expiry date.

In the same way car insurance works between two parties, options are a contract between two parties, a seller and a buyer. The option seller is selling the buyer the right to buy or sell a stock at a certain price point, while the option buyer is acquiring the right to buy or sell a stock at a certain price. Each contract that the buyer and seller agree upon applies to 100 shares of the underlying stock. So, if you sell 10 contracts, you are agreeing on a contract for 1,000 shares of the underlying company's stock.

The buyer of a stock option pays a premium to (for an obligation from) the seller. Regardless of whether it is a Call or a Put option, the option buyer acquires a right and pays a premium; the option seller assumes an obligation and collects the premium from the buyer. It is as you would expect: when you buy something, you pay for it; when you sell something, you collect money for it.

Just like there is a market to buy and sell stocks, a stock market, and a market to buy and sell insurance, there is also a market to buy and sell stock options. Your stockbroker can provide you with access to a stock options trading platform, referred to as an "option chain," that will enable you to trade in the stock options market.

TWO REASONS YOU MAY WANT TO PARTAKE IN SELLING CALLS AND PUTS:

The two main reasons you may want to sell Call options:

- To earn high levels of income by collecting premiums.

- To potentially sell a stock you already own at a price above the current market price; an ideal situation, would be to sell a call option when you own a stock that you believe will be over-valued at the strike price.

The two main reasons you may want to sell Put options:

- To earn high levels of income by collecting premiums.

- To potentially buy a desired stock at a price below the current market price; an ideal situation would be to sell a put option when you believe owning the stock at the strike price would be a compelling value.

INITIATING AN OPTIONS CONTRACT

Each options trade involves two steps: opening the trade and closing the trade. Selling (instead of buying) stock options to open a trade is what I do. This means you will be the one selling the right to a buyer and collecting a premium. (When you sell options, you are assuming the same position as the insurance company in the transaction.) "Sell to open" is also what I recommend others do. As time passes, assuming a constant stock price, the value of an option will decrease as the expiry date approaches. You want to be a net seller, not buyer, of depreciating assets. So, we will solely talk about the strategy of "selling to open" here as it is a more conservative approach than "buying to open." The trade will close either upon the expiry of the contract length or upon "buying to close" the option prior to the expiration of the contract.

The option seller uses the option chain to select a stock name, contract type (Call or Put), strike price, expiration date, and the number of contracts that you want to sell. When you submit a "sell to open" order for Call or Put option contracts, the option chain will provide quotes with the value of the premiums based on your selected parameters. When the order is filled, the option seller receives confirmation and collects the premiums instantly, and the premium is deposited directly into the seller's account.

After selling the option, if the stock price remains below a Call option's strike price or above a Put option's strike price, the option will be "out-of-the-money" and the contract will expire worthless at the expiration date, but the option seller will keep the premium payment, much like a car insurance company keeps your premium payments even if nothing happens to your car. The option buyer was protected by the insurance if the buyer needed to use it, but for the duration of the contract term, nothing happened in which the buyer needed to exercise it. Stocks are not assigned if the trade is out-of-the-money—the Call buyer does not "call" for the stock from the option seller, nor does a Put buyer "put" the stock to the option seller. When the option is out-of-the-money, an option buyer will not exercise their right because the option buyer can buy or sell the stock more profitably in the stock market.

Therefore, when options expire out-of-the-money, the option seller not only gets to keep the collected premiums but also gets to keep the stock or cash that was used to secure the now expired option contracts. The option seller can then sell new option contracts using the same stock or cash that was used to secure the expired options, collecting additional premiums at whatever rates are available. Each time the contracts expire out of the money, you can continue repeating this process to generate income. A potential downside if your Puts continually expire out-of-the-money is you may miss your chance of owning a winner, but you get to keep all your premiums and the cash that was used to secure the put contracts.

What happens when a contract expires "in the money"?

With Calls, if the stock price reaches or exceeds the strike price at any time on or before the expiration date, the Call's strike price is "in-the-money."

When that happens, the option seller still keeps the premium payments but will be obligated to sell their stock to the option buyer at the strike price. The stock sale is typically additional profit for the option seller because Call strike prices are usually set higher than the stock prices were when the trade was opened. The potential downside is the option seller will miss out on any stock price appreciation upside that exists beyond the strike price when the stocks are assigned.

With Puts, if the stock price declines to the strike price or lower at any time on or before the expiration date, the Puts' strike price will then be "in-the-money." When this happens, the Put option seller will still keep the premium payments generated by selling to open the contract but will be obligated to buy the stock from the option buyer at the strike price. Put strike prices are usually set lower than what the stock price was when the option seller sold the Put, but the potential downside is the Put option seller will have to buy the stock at a higher, less profitable price than what the stock price is when the stock is assigned. You buy the stock at the Puts' strike price and miss the opportunity to buy the stock even cheaper.

COST BASIS VERSUS ASSIGNMENT COSTS

The premiums collected to open the Puts that were assigned will be deducted from the strike price paid to purchase the shares at assignment, and your brokerage will list the difference (the strike price minus the collected premiums) as the cost basis for the assigned shares. In addition to cost basis, you should keep track of "assignment costs." The assignment cost is equal to the strike price when shares were bought or sold at assignment and excludes any benefits to the cost or sales basis from the premiums collected. The Put assignment cost is therefore higher than the cost basis for the assigned shares.

REAL LIFE EXAMPLES

Theory can be boring and confusing. I sold options to build a position in NU. Let's look at the NU trades to explain how and why selling options can be a better way to build a position than buying the stock directly.

Although NU has an attractive business model, there was more than a normal amount of uncertainty when I decided to add NU to the buy-and-hold collection. The business became publicly traded at the end of 2021 (NU is new), has only been profitable since the second half of 2022, and NU's stock price rose rapidly right before the decision was made to purchase shares. All other stock names in the buy-and-hold collection were initially purchased directly in the stock market. Given the uncertainty around NU, I decided to use options to build a position in NU instead of buying stock directly. The table below summarizes all the NU option contracts opened in 2023.

NU Holdings (Nubank) - Option Contracts Opened in 2023

Trade Sets	Dates		Stock Price		Contract				Premiums (per share)		Duration (Days)		Net Premiums at Close		
	Opened Trade	Closed Trade	At Open	At Close	Type	Number	Expiration Date	Strike Price	Open	Close	Open	Close	Gains or Loss ($)	Annualized ($)	Annualized (%)
1	16-Jun-23	13-Jul-23	$7.47	$8.07	Puts	150	21-Jul-23	$7.00	0.16	(0.03)	35	27	$1,950	$26,361	25.58%
2	10-Jul-23	10-Aug-23	$7.84	$7.96	Puts	200	11-Aug-23	$7.50	0.24	(0.03)	32	31	$4,208	$49,546	33.98%
3	11-Jul-23	4-Aug-23	$7.79	$7.96	Puts	200	4-Aug-23	$7.50	0.19		24	24	$3,800	$57,792	39.53%
4	13-Jul-23	11-Aug-23	$8.24	$7.96	Puts	150	11-Aug-23	$8.00	0.27		29	29	$4,050	$50,974	43.96%
5	24-Jul-23	18-Aug-23	$7.84	$7.21	Puts	200	18-Aug-23	$7.50	0.26		25	25	$5,200	$75,920	52.43%
6	4-Aug-23	15-Sep-23	$7.96	$7.36	Puts	200	15-Sep-23	$8.00	0.48		42	42	$9,600	$83,429	55.47%
7	14-Aug-23	1-Sep-23	$7.94	$7.08	Calls	150	20-Oct-23	$8.00	0.62	(0.14)	67	18	$7,200	$146,000	130.47%
8	16-Aug-23	25-Aug-23	$7.99	$7.00	Puts	200	25-Aug-23	$8.00	0.25		9	9	$5,000	$202,778	130.82%
9	16-Aug-23	8-Sep-23	$7.85	$6.83	Puts	200	8-Sep-23	$7.50	0.18		23	23	$3,625	$57,527	39.30%
10	21-Aug-23	1-Sep-23	$7.32	$7.09	Calls	200	22-Sep-23	$8.00	0.14	(0.03)	32	11	$2,200	$73,000	50.62%
11	28-Aug-23	20-Oct-23	$6.77	$8.17	Calls	200	20-Oct-23	$8.00	0.11		53	53	$2,220	$15,289	11.49%
12	1-Sep-23	19-Jan-24	$7.02		Calls	195	19-Jan-24	$8.00	0.45		140	140	$8,802	$22,949	17.92%
13	5-Sep-23	19-Jan-24	$6.87		Calls	200	19-Jan-24	$8.00	0.41		136	136	$8,200	$22,007	17.03%
14	5-Sep-23	13-Oct-23	$6.84	$7.76	Calls	150	13-Oct-23	$7.50	0.16		38	38	$2,346	$22,534	22.48%
15	11-Sep-23	6-Oct-23	$7.18	$7.37	Calls	200	6-Oct-23	$7.50	0.17		25	25	$3,400	$49,640	35.43%
16	14-Sep-23	26-Oct-23	$7.55	$7.88	Puts	200	27-Oct-23	$7.50	0.36	(0.02)	43	42	$6,794	$59,043	41.23%
17	9-Oct-23	10-Nov-23	$7.26	$8.52	Calls	200	10-Nov-23	$7.50	0.27		32	32	$5,400	$61,594	44.09%
18	16-Oct-23	17-Nov-23	$7.78	$7.37	Puts	200	17-Nov-23	$7.00	0.16		32	32	$3,200	$36,500	26.68%
19	19-Oct-23	10-Nov-23	$8.20	$8.57	Puts	200	1-Dec-23	$8.00	0.36	(0.17)	43	22	$3,800	$63,045	40.36%
20	23-Oct-23	14-Nov-23	$8.20	$8.66	Puts	200	17-Nov-23	$8.00	0.31	(0.10)	25	22	$4,228	$70,146	45.03%
21	26-Oct-23	14-Nov-23	$7.91	$8.81	Puts	200	17-Nov-23	$7.50	0.22	(0.04)	22	19	$3,600	$69,158	47.24%
22	10-Nov-23	29-Dec-23	$8.52	$8.33	Calls	200	29-Dec-23	$9.50	0.16		49	49	$3,200	$23,837	14.26%
23	15-Nov-23	15-Dec-23	$7.99	$8.30	Puts	200	15-Dec-23	$8.00	0.33		30	30	$6,600	$80,300	52.35%
24	16-Nov-23	8-Dec-23	$8.05	$8.32	Puts	200	8-Dec-23	$8.00	0.25		22	22	$5,000	$82,955	53.52%
25	17-Nov-23	19-Jan-24	$8.03		Puts	200	19-Jan-24	$8.00	0.41		63	63	$8,200	$47,508	31.30%
26	6-Dec-23	5-Jan-24	$8.21		Puts	200	5-Jan-24	$8.00	0.21		30	30	$4,200	$51,100	32.80%
27	11-Dec-23	12-Jan-24	$8.19		Puts	200	12-Jan-24	$8.00	0.21		32	32	$4,200	$47,906	30.75%
28	15-Dec-23	26-Jan-24	$8.32		Puts	200	26-Jan-24	$8.00	0.20		42	42	$4,000	$34,762	22.28%
29	18-Dec-23	16-Feb-24	$8.33		Puts	200	16-Feb-24	$8.00	0.28		60	60	$5,600	$34,067	22.06%

Current Date: 31-Dec-23 $8.33

Total Duration: 199   Contracts Open: 1,395

Total Net Premiums Collected: $139,823 $256,460   36.98%

Average value of cash and stock at risk selling NU options: $693,563

NU stock options were sold starting in June 2023 in a tax-deferred account. Let's break-down the first trade for clarity.

- As you can see from the table, the first trade was sold to open on June 16, 2023. The stock price was $7.47 when 150 put option contracts were sold to open with a strike price of $7.00 and an expiration date of July 21, 2023.

- The premiums collected at open were $0.16 per share. Each option contract applies to 100 shares, so the 150 contracts apply to 15,000 shares of stock. The premium amount collected at open was $2,400 (0.16 multiplied by 15,000).

- The 150 Puts obligated the seller (me) to purchase 15,000 shares of NU at $7 per share on or before the expiration date of July 21, 2023. The contract duration at open is 35 days-to-expiration, the time from June 16 through July 21.

- The 150 contracts were bought to close early, on July 13, 2023, at a cost of $0.03 per share, when the stock price was $8.07 per share. The contract duration at close was 27 days.

- No shares were purchased because the stock price remained higher than the Puts' $7 strike price.

- The net premiums collected per share were $0.13 for the closed contracts (the difference between the $0.16 per share collected at open and the $0.03 paid at close).

- The net premium collected at close for a 27-day commitment was $1,950 ($0.13 per share multiplied by 15,000 shares) and is a yield of 1.9% on the $103,050 of cash value at risk (15,000 shares multiplied by a $7 strike price per share minus the $1,950 net premium collected at close).

- If you annualize the net premium earned, it equates to $26,361 ($1,950 divided by 27 days multiplied by 365 days per year).

- The annualized return for the closed trade was a 25.58% CAGR ($26,361 divided by the $103,050 value at risk).

The second trade sold to open 200 Puts on July 10, 2023, and so on. Multiple trades were usually open at the same time. Some of the Puts later expired in the money, and the shares were assigned, meaning it resulted in me purchasing the shares. I purchased the assigned shares at the Puts' strike price. Calls were sold to open using some of the newly purchased shares. As you can see in the table, a total of twenty-nine NU option trades were opened in 2023. Twenty-two trades were closed in 2023 and seven trades were still open at year-end. The stock price at year-end was $8.33 per share.

Using options to build a position in NU was more lucrative than if I had bought the stock directly:

- Selling NU options collected net premiums of $139,823. The value at risk (cash or stock value) averaged $693,563 for the 199-day duration, from June 16 until December 31.

- When you annualize the premiums collected, it equates to $256,460 per year (139,823 divided by 199 days and multiplied by 365 days per year) earned on a $693,563 average value at risk. The annualized return is a 37% compound annual growth rate (256,460/693,563).

- In addition to the premiums collected, 73,800 NU shares were purchased, when Puts were assigned, at an assignment cost of $8.00 per share (the assignment cost per share excludes any benefits from premiums collected). The premium gains equate to $1.89 per share (139,823/73,800).

- If you deduct the premium gains of $1.89 per share from the assignment cost of $8.00 per share, it equates to an effective cost of $6.11 per share, or effectively 27% below the year-end stock price.

- The stock price rose during the same period, but only 12% from $7.47 to $8.33 at year-end. The stock price averaged $7.79 per share and the range was a low of $6.80 to a high of $8.82 per share.

The reason to bother with selling options at all is because, as shown in the actual NU example above, it can be very lucrative; a 37% compound annual growth rate is much more lucrative than what you can reasonably expect over time from investing in stocks, bonds, real estate, or other investment alternatives. The plan is to both continue to hold NU shares for capital appreciation as well as to continue to sell options with NU.

We have two more options basics to address before we get to the selling options strategy.

COVERED CALLS AND CASH-SECURED PUTS

Selling "covered Calls" or "cash-secured Puts," means you will need to have sufficient stock or cash in your account while the options are open to sell or purchase the stock should the buyer of the Calls or Puts exercise his right to "call" or "put" the shares from or to you.

- When 200 NU Puts with a $8 per share strike price are sold to open, the same account has to have sufficient cash ($160,000) available to purchase 20,000 shares of NU stock at the $8 per share strike price if the Puts become in-the-money.

- Or, alternatively, if you sold to open 200 NU covered Calls, that means you must already own 20,000 shares of NU stock to cover the Calls you sold to open. Those 'cover' shares need to be in the same account and will be sold at the strike price you selected if the Calls' cover shares get assigned prior to or on the expiration date.

DELTA AND IMPLIED VOLATILITY

The option chain also includes useful analytics. There are lots of analytics. Much of it is confusing, but a lot of it can be ignored. Some of the metrics are referred to as 'Greeks'. The two analytics that you will most frequently use are Delta and Implied Volatility (IV). The Delta for the NU Puts sold on June 16, 2023, were listed in the option chain as 0.2744 and the implied volatility was listed as 42%.

Delta is the amount an option price is expected to move based on a $1 change in the underlying stock. If a call has a Delta of 0.50 and the stock goes up $1, in theory, the price of the call will go up about $0.50. If the stock goes down $1, in theory, the price of the call will go down about $0.50. Delta's true definition is useful to know, but another way to think about Delta is as the probability an option will wind up in-the-money at expiration. Technically, this is not a valid definition because the actual math behind Delta is not a probability calculation. The future is uncertain, and Delta is at best an approximate probability. However, it is viewed as a "roughly right" proxy for probability, and Delta is frequently referred to as probability in the options world.

A Delta of 0.50 will often be referenced as a 50% probability. The NU Puts on June 16, 2023, with a $7 strike price and a 0.2744 Delta would be referenced as a contract with a 27% chance of expiring in-the-money, or there is a 27% chance the shares will be assigned to the option seller at $7 per share on or before the expiration date. The option seller will collect higher (more lucrative) premiums when a strike price is selected with a higher Delta because there is a greater chance the stock price will be in the money and that shares will be assigned.

Implied Volatility (IV) is a different analytic but also important. Implied Volatility is the market's view of the likely movement in an individual stock name's future stock price. Implied Volatility is often viewed as a proxy of market risk—higher risk has a higher implied volatility—and is one of the deciding factors in the pricing of options. Implied Volatility is not the same as actual, historical volatility (also known as realized volatility), which measures past market changes and their actual results.

Selling options on stocks that have higher implied volatility will allow you to collect more lucrative premium payments than selling options on stocks with lower implied volatility. As an example, selling options with the highly volatile Tesla stock will be much more lucrative than if you use the much less volatile Berkshire stock. On June 27, 2022, if you sold Puts that committed you to purchase a million dollars of Tesla shares at a strike price that has a 0.30 delta with an expiration date of July 15, the implied volatility would be 72% and you would collect a premium of $35,000 in exchange for making that 18 days-to-expiration commitment. In contrast, selling Puts that committed you to purchase a million dollars of Berkshire shares at a 0.30 delta with the same expiration date would have an implied volatility of 25 percent and would pay you only $13,000. Big differences in implied volatility equate to big differences in the amount of premiums you can collect.

Implied volatilities are different for different stocks, but they also change dynamically over time for the same stock. When the underlying stock approaches an earnings announcement, implied volatilities will likely rise because of the uncertainty that exists prior to the announcement. After the earnings are announced, the implied volatilities will then often decline. As another example, if the broader market slumps rapidly because of some negative event or sentiment, implied volatilities will likely increase as well.

Now you know what an option is, that there are two types (Calls or Puts), and that they can be sold or bought. We've also covered how options work in general and reviewed some actual trade results from selling options to highlight the financial returns that are possible. If stock options are new to you, this is a lot to get your head around. Feel free to soak it all in before moving on to a description of the recommended options selling strategy.

LOOK FOR INSIGHTS BY INVERSION

When you sell options, you should still follow Warren Buffet's advice: Don't lose money. You should protect the value of what you already have, plus collect generous premiums that generate income no matter which way the market trends. You should also avoid any unnecessary complexity that can suck-up tons of time and energy.

The issue is there are lots of alternative option trading strategies you can learn about and deploy that are not what you want to do. Many option trading strategies that are taught are overly complicated. Some strategies assume you can predict short-term market movements, but no one is likely to do that reliably. Many will pose risks to your existing wealth or have big payoffs but with very low probabilities of success.

The world of stock options can be risky and complex. You will want to understand what matters and follow a well-defined strategy for selling options.

When Charlie Munger wanted to learn complex topics and understand how and why they work, he usually started by using inversion in the intense manner counseled by Carl Gustav Jacob Jacobi, the great algebraist: "invert, always invert." Charlie was a big proponent of inversion because it works so well. Complex problems frequently get—Charlie would have even said "usually are"—easier to solve if you turn them around in reverse. Restating the problem in inverse form clarifies thinking and a solution often comes more easily.

It is not enough to think about complex topics and difficult problems in one way. Instead of only looking for how to succeed, first make a list of how to fail, identifying what you want to avoid. Being a student of other people's folly—studying where people go astray and why things don't work—can serve you well. Ponder in an intense manner on the specific topic and gain some experience to identify what would be the worst outcomes and then how you could avoid them. Define a plan that avoids your worst outcomes, and you may find your path to success, without even having to grasp many of the esoteric aspects that too often accompany complex topics.

Inversion is counterintuitive for many. Spending time thinking about the opposite of what you want doesn't come naturally for most people. And yet Charlie and many of the smartest people in history made the effort to learn and habitually apply inversion because it works so well.

"If a man will begin with certainties, he shall end in doubts; but if he will be content to begin with doubts he shall end in certainties."
— Sir Francis Bacon

Let's try a bit of inversion now. Stock options are complex and how to trade them well is a difficult problem to solve. Let's develop a strategy for trading stock options by using inversion. The first step is to identify common things you will want to avoid when trading options or, said another way, identify the common things you will not do when trading options.

Below is list of actions, that occur regularly in the options world, that you **should not do** when you trade options.

1. Buy to open options.

2. Use margin (also called borrowed money, debt or leverage).

3. Predict future near-term stock price movements.

4. Realize capital losses.

5. Close unprofitable trades, realizing cash losses.

6. Realize other cash losses.

7. Deficient performance monitoring

You may be thinking that is quite a list of big rocks, things you should avoid or not do, and it is. One of the reasons inverting works so well is because humans are wired to find threats. You now need to define a plan that avoids the big rocks. You will gain a solid understanding of what matters and be on your way towards creating a winning strategy.

1. Sell to open options. Do not buy to open.

2. Do not use margin. Only sell covered Calls and/or cash secured Puts.

3. Stay Uncertain about future near-term stock price movements. Do not try to predict near-term market direction. Sell to open an options trade only when all scenarios are acceptable.

4. **Protect Equity Risked.** To avoid realizing capital losses, select Call strike prices that are at or above the assignment cost (or at or above the cost basis when shares were purchased directly) for the shares being used to cover the Calls.

5. **Close Profitable Trades.** Buy to close early, prior to expiry, only when the cost to close is less than the amount collected when opened, otherwise allow open contracts to expire and accept assignments if they occur.

6. Avoid or minimize other cash losses. Sell options in tax advantaged accounts, avoid margin interest, earn competitive interest rates on cash and on cash being used to secure Puts, and minimize other transactional costs.

7. Track results. Keep sufficient records to enable accurate performance monitoring.

SELLING OPTIONS STRATEGY, SUPER-CPT

Those seven elements form the basis for the recommended options trading strategy, named the **SUPER-CPT** selling options strategy (**S**tay **U**ncertain, **P**rotect **E**quity **R**isked, and **C**lose **P**rofitable **T**rades). The strategy only sells covered call and cash-secured put options with stocks you own or want to own for the long-term, selects strike prices at or above assignment cost to avoid realizing capital losses, and collects profitable net premiums on each trade, and it does all of that without you having to be able to predict near-term stock price movements.

Utilizing this inverted plan will also greatly simplify what you need to learn about options since much of what happens in the options trading world is now no longer relevant if you do not buy to open, do not use margin, do not try to predict near-term stock price movements, and you are willing to accept assignments. This inverted approach will have lower risks and require much less time and effort than many of the options trading strategies that are commonly taught. The complex and risky options world is greatly reduced to a simpler, safer subset of activities.

When using SUPER-CPT, you only sell options on stocks that you already own or want to own: stocks of good businesses that you believe will continue to grow their intrinsic business value over the long-term and that you are willing to hold for as long as they remain good businesses. Stock selection methodology is therefore the same as what was already covered for buy-and-hold investments.

If you could predict near-term stock price movements, you would sell Calls on a stock when you believe the stock will go down (when you have a bearish view) and sell Puts when you believe the stock will go up (bullish) but, in the real world, some things are unpredictable. Near-term stock price movements are unpredictable. We just cannot know. Instead of placing a bet on a hunch about a discrete, time-limited stock price direction, consider the possible stock price scenarios (a stock can only go down, up, or stay flat during the contracted duration) and only sell to open options at a selected strike price when any of the possible scenarios are acceptable to you.

You should select Call strike prices that are at or above the assignment costs of your cover shares and when you are willing to sell the cover shares at the strike price. You should only select Put strike prices that are low enough that you would be willing to buy more shares at the strike price. If any scenario is unacceptable, you should not sell the option. You will often decide to have both Calls and Puts open at the same time on the same stock, collecting double premiums, because you are neutral and uncertain about the market's near-term direction. Once open contracts are closed early or expired, you use the same stock or cash to cover or secure the "sell to open" of new options again, and you collect more premiums, repeatedly, for as long as you can continue to find acceptable strike prices.

Your primary objectives using SUPER-CPT are: 1.) to protect the value of capital (also called equity or stocks) at risk that is being used to cover call option contracts by selecting Call strike prices that are at or above the assignment cost for the shares being used to cover the Calls (or at or above the cost basis when cover shares were purchased directly); 2.) only buy to close a trade early if the cost to close is less than the amount collected when it was opened, otherwise allow open contracts to expire and accept any assignments if they occur; 3.) maximize the annualized returns from net premiums collected by repeatedly selling option contracts, maximizing the annualized returns on the value at risk dedicated to selling options.

That third objective, maximizing the annualized returns from net premiums collected, is only an objective if the first two objectives are met.

You should select longer Call durations when necessary to select a strike price high enough to be at or above the assignment cost of shares used to cover Calls. The annualized returns will be lower for longer duration contracts than they would be for shorter duration contracts, but you will still collect positive premiums, the returns are often still good, and sometimes longer is necessary to find strike prices high enough to allow you to avoid the risk of a capital loss. Be patient when necessary to avoid risking capital losses. Avoiding the potential for capital losses will be worth the wait. You do not want to be incentivized to buy stocks at high prices and sell stocks at lower prices, but you will be if you only look at maximizing premiums and neglect the potential for capital losses.

When you ponder on it, those objectives yield a low-risk approach. The first objective ensures you will have no realized capital losses when call options are assigned, and the underlying shares are sold at the strike price, protecting your equity at risk. The second objective results in each closed trade being profitable, meaning your trades will not realize any net cash losses. Avoiding the losses with the first two objectives really helps your overall results. You are not digging a hole that needs to be filled with net premiums just to reach a break-even. All net premiums collected, the third objective, will become gains. The amount of net premiums collected will vary for each underlying stock name and will depend on what happens in the market and with the business but with a diverse collection of stock names the premiums collected (earned) can be steady and quite generous (large amounts) overall.

RETURN TARGETS

My return target for selling options is to earn at least a 20% CAGR on the total value at risk (stocks and cash) being used to sell options. Net premiums collected will likely be the bulk of your returns. For simplicity, imagine for a base case that the net premiums collected from selling options are targeted to yield more than 20% returns on the average value at risk without realizing any capital losses nor collecting any dividends. If you make a bit less from premiums but make up for it by realizing capital gains (or by collecting dividends while selling options) and that results in more than a 20% CAGR, that will work too. Either outcome would meet the target: 1.) more than 20% annual gains on the average total value at risk from just the net premiums collected with no realized capital gains nor dividends OR 2.) some combination of net premiums collected, realized capital gains, and collected dividends at more than 20% gains annually on the average total value at risk.

Most of your stock gains as a buy-and-hold investor come during short, and unexpected, upward bursts in the stock price. Those positive events do not happen often, and it is impossible to predict when they will happen. Buy-and-hold investing will do better than selling options when the stock has a quick and large upward price movement, but even the stocks of good businesses will move downwards, sideways, or oscillate up and down for very extended periods, even years, and during those times, returns from selling options can be much better than from buy-and-hold investing.

You will love collecting premiums, but you will not want to give up completely on stock price gains that may occur beyond a Calls' strike price and you also will not want to lose all your shares, so you should hold some shares long. Your shares held long will participate in any stock price gains that may occur beyond the selected Call strike prices (should there be a large, rapid gain in stock price). The consequence is that you should generally have three target buckets for each stock name in your selling options portfolio:

1.) Shares Held Long:

2.) Shares used as Cover for Call Options:

3.) Cash to Secure Put Options.

The number of shares held long, bucket 1, stays relatively constant since it represents your buy-and-hold position in the stock name. You should want to own these shares for decades. Over time, you want these to become low cost-basis shares. When the worst case happens, the stock price jumps out the window and falls well below your open puts' strike prices, the low-cost basis shares being held long can soften the blow emotionally. The value of shares held long are not included in the value at risk selling options; their performance remains within the buy-and-hold collection.

The last two buckets can be very dynamic. If the stock price falls and all your Puts get assigned, you will have more shares and too many Calls for a while (and perhaps even no Puts for a while). When that happens, you can get more aggressive with half of the Calls by still selecting strike prices above assignment cost but at higher Deltas until you are no longer above your target level of cover shares. Alternatively, if the stock price rises a lot and quickly, the opposite happens: you will lose your cover shares, will have more cash from the proceeds of the sold cover shares, and should then get more aggressive with half of the Puts until you return to your target level of cover shares. Having shares held long, in the first bucket, enables you to be more emotionally comfortable and that will support your effort to sell options rationally with buckets 2 and 3.

You should close trades early only when it is profitable. Many times, when you buy to close early, it is because the stock price has moved in your favor, and you have earned the bulk of the premiums in a smaller fraction of the contract duration. When that happens, buying to close the trade early will boost the closed trade's return higher than it was at open and that is a good thing. You should buy to close an open trade early when it will improve the trade's rate of return and you are ready to redeploy the cash or stock to a new trade.

Once contracts expire, or are closed, sell new options again, earn more premiums, and generate income continuously. If you avoid margin, are willing to allow assignments to happen, and you are willing to switch between selling Calls and Puts, when the stock price remains relatively close to your strike at expiration, it is not an issue at all. There is no need to waste money buying to close, simply allow it to expire, and allow it to be assigned should it happen to expire in the money.

SUPER-CPT when combined with a buy-and-hold investing strategy can have higher returns, building your wealth more effectively than if you were to only do buy-and-hold investing. It allows you to consistently invest in high-quality businesses that you want to own for the long term, and at the same time, it allows you to earn additional income from collecting generous premiums by selling options with those same underlying stocks. For such a low-risk strategy, SUPER-CPT can be very lucrative and much more rewarding than if you only do buy-and-hold investing.

WORST CASE SCENARIO

What happens in the worst case using SUPER-CPT? The worst case is when the stock price moves against your open Puts in a major way, a large stock price drop. When that happens, and it will happen, you should:

1. Still allow that trade to expire. The SUPER-CPT investor abides the market. Buying to close in that situation would be unprofitable. It would be a negative net premium collected for that trade if you bought to close, and you do not take the certain cash loss. By allowing the trade to expire instead, it will remain a profitable trade since you would have collected a premium to open the trade and you would not pay anything to buy to close it.

2. After the prior step, you will have collected positive net premiums, but the Puts will expire in-the-money and the shares will be assigned to you at the strike price. You will have an unrealized capital loss since

the stock price will now be below your assignment cost.

3. You then use the newly assigned shares as cover to sell Call options and collect more premiums, but if the stock fell very low, selecting a high enough Call strike price may require a much longer than normal days-to-expiration contract, or

4. In the worst case, you may have to pause selling Call options until the stock price recovers.

In that worst case, when you must pause selling Call options with those shares until the stock price recovers, the situation is back to being like a buy-and-hold investment. Time should be your friend and you should rely on it instead of selecting a Call strike price below your assignment cost that would risk realizing a capital loss. The cumulative positive net premiums that you already collected should provide some comfort and hopefully help you to be emotionally patient.

The risk of big stock price movements against your open option positions will be an issue (big price movements downwards are also an issue with stock investing). The risk of a big stock price move has some tactical consequences:

- When you sell to open a Put, a lower Delta usually does not allow you to select a much lower Put strike price, just a little bit lower. Therefore, your risk of a big move still exists with both a low (less than 0.20) or a high Delta (close to 0.50).

- Avoid selling to open Puts with short durations because the premiums will be smaller, and it is like picking up pennies in front of a steamroller. You want a bigger reward for taking the risk of getting squashed. As a guideline, the shortest duration you should select when you sell to open a Put is probably 3 weeks, but the average duration at open for the SUPERCPT test has been 49 days thus far.

- You should actively create option diversity – option type (have both Calls and Puts open), dates opened, strike price, days-to-expiration, and stock names.

- Break up your option trades into smaller sets, to ensure value-at-risk is not too large for a single trade and to allow you to diversify over time. Sell to open some this week, next week. When there is a big stock move up, sell to open some Calls, then sell to open Puts when the stock price has a major move down, and so on. You are not predicting future stock movements, only taking advantage of big stock price movements that have happened to open a diverse group of trades.

- You also should keep a level of cash to give you freedom to take advantage if you see big volatility.

- If the stock price is well below your independently derived intrinsic value and you want to own more shares to hold long, you should simply buy the shares instead of selling Puts; you should also not sell to open Calls when you believe the stock price is well below your value estimate. "Well below" seldom happens. If the stock price is reasonable versus your intrinsic value, you should sell Puts in the manner that was shown to build the position in NU earlier in this section. When the stock price is overvalued, well above your intrinsic value estimate, you should not sell to open Puts with that stock name. Use that cash to sell to open Puts with a different stock name or wait for conditions to change.

Note that in a discrete worst possible case, a very large stock price drop that goes well below your Puts' strike price, the SUPER-CPT method will have the same risks as a buy-and-hold investment. With SUPER-CPT in all other cases, you are collecting positive net premiums but giving up some potential stock price upside versus buy-and-hold investing.

You may be asking, are the cumulative positive net premiums collected from selling options worth more than giving up some potential stock price upside? That is an excellent question. Based on my experience thus far, the cumulative premiums collected are worth more than the potential stock price upside that you give up.

The cumulative net premiums collected from selling options are much more lucrative than I imagined they would be. Let's review SUPER-CPT's actual performance results so that you can reach your own conclusion.

SUPER-CPT PERFORMANCE RESULTS

Results from the conservative strategy, SUPER-CPT, have exceeded expectations. SUPER-CPT has been used exclusively with four underlying stocks to test out the strategy. The strategy started with PubMatic on November 22, 2022, Eaton on April 6, 2023, American Express on April 20, 2023, and NU on June 15, 2023. Both Calls and Puts were sold, and often both types were open at the same time on the same underlying stock. Each Call strike price was selected at or above assignment cost, protecting the equity being risked. Each closed trade collected positive net premiums, protecting the cash at risk. Or, said another way, I did not buy to close any trade at a higher cost than what was collected to open the trade.

For the SUPER-CPT test, a total of 82 trades (each trade consisting of multiple contracts) were opened, 67 were closed, and 15 trades remained open at year-end 2023. The days-to-expiration averaged 49 days at open and 44 days for the closed trades. The test has resulted in 24 assignments out of the 67 closed trades, or 36%. The average delta for the 67 trades closed was 0.3591. (It would often be referenced as 36% in the options world.) Delta and the percentage of assignments were essentially the same number, so delta has correlated well with probability of being assigned.

The SUPER-CPT test results are from November 2022 through year-end 2023. The net premiums collected yielded a 31% CAGR on the average value at risk (cash or stock value being used to sell options), plus there were no capital losses realized. Some dividends were collected while selling options with the same shares, but the dividend amounts were relatively small, and when added to the net premiums collected, the 31% CAGR remained the same. Only realized gains and realized losses are included in performance results. A stock loss or gain only becomes realized after you sell the shares. You realize a capital loss when you sell stock at prices below the price you paid to purchase those same shares. You realize a capital gain when you sell stock at prices above the price you paid to purchase those same shares. Unrealized gains and unrealized losses are also tracked and the net unrealized sum at year-end 2023 for the SUPER-CPT selling options portfolio was positive (an unrealized gain) and within 1% of the average value at risk.

The 31% CAGR earned with SUPER-CPT is well above the 20% target for selling options, and it is as good as my overall selling options results of 30% CAGR, which includes more aggressive and more active strategies than SUPER-CPT. Based on the positive experience, the use of SUPER-CPT has been expanded beyond the stock names in the test, increasing the value at risk operating under SUPER-CPT. Performance results will continue to be tracked. Updates will be included in future editions of Wealthy & Wise.

Recall that the historical long-term average compound annual growth rates (CAGRs) for various assets and investing strategies are as follows, in nominal values (not adjusted for inflation):

- Bonds and US Treasuries at 4-5% CAGR.
- Average stock investor at less than 6% CAGR.

- Savings deposited consistently into a very low-cost index fund, 7-9% CAGR.
- Overall US stock market at 10% CAGR.
- A collection of long-term, buy-and-hold investments in good businesses at 15% CAGR.

The buy-and-hold collection's target is a 15% CAGR, but selling options with SUPER-CPT has lower risks and a higher return target, at more than a 20% CAGR. "What's the catch?" you may be asking.

WHAT'S THE CATCH?

The catch is that you do need to have money saved that can be fully dedicated to selling options. You do not need a huge amount of money, but even moderate amounts of money can be difficult to accumulate when you are young or just starting to save. You also need to invest in individual stock names, be comfortable with a buy-and-hold stock investing methodology, and make the effort to learn how to sell stock options without using margin. I mentioned earlier that most people invest in mutual funds instead of individual stock names. Of the few that do invest in individual stocks, even fewer utilize a buy-and-hold methodology.

WHAT'S DIFFERENT ABOUT SUPER-CPT?

What is different about SUPER-CPT compared to other selling options methodologies? I already mentioned that most traders try to predict near-term stock price movements and many buy, instead of sell, to open an options trade. SUPER-CPT does neither of those. An even more striking SUPER-CPT difference that would stand out to a professional trader is the large number of assignments and how few trades were bought to close early, prior to the expiry date. Buying to close early is frequently a large cost for professional traders, but it happens because professional traders use margin and do not want to get assigned since getting assigned usually would require tapping into expensive and risky margin.

Unlike SUPER-CPT, professional traders close early almost all of their trades, prior to the expiration date. A professional trader's common rule of thumb is to buy to close their trades at a 50-75% profit or no less than 21 days to expiration, whichever occurs first. The NU trades that were reviewed earlier use SUPER-CPT and you can see that only 8 of 22 closed trades (36%) were bought to close early, and each of those closed trades were profitable. The bulk, 64%, of the NU trades were held until the contracts expired and that is much different than what is normally done.

Because margin use when trading options is so prevalent, it is just assumed in most materials. The bulk of what is taught in external courses is how to trade options using margin. Trading tools also make the same margin-use assumption.

I want to highlight how an option chain trade order form makes a margin-use assumption. This time the stock name is Eaton (another stock name in the buy-and-hold collection) and the action is to sell to open 13 call options.

- The buy-and-hold collection owns Eaton shares with a low cost basis, purchased eleven years ago in a tax advantaged account, for $36.96 per share. With Eaton's stock price at $245 per share on January 19, 2024, the stock's compound annual growth rate has been a 19% CAGR for eleven years, excluding dividends that were received during the eleven years.

- If you used those same 1,300 shares to sell to open 13 covered Calls with a $250 strike and 56 days-to-expiration, you would collect a premium of $9,165.

- If the stock price stays below your strike for the duration of the Calls, you keep the premiums, your realized gain would be $9,165, and you would retain your cover shares.

- If instead the stock price moves above the strike prior to or on expiry and the shares are assigned (sold at the strike price), you still keep the $9,165 premium, plus you realize a large capital gain compared to your cost basis, a $276,952 capital gain ($250 minus cost basis of $36.96 multiplied by 1,300 shares). Your combined gain would be $286,177 when compared to your cost basis.

- Alternatively, if you compared your outcome to the stock price of $244.60 per share when the Calls were opened, you would also have a stock price gain, a $7,020 gain (250 minus 244.60 multiplied by 1,300 shares), plus you would still have the collected premiums of $9,165 for a total gain of $16,185, when compared to the stock price at the time the option trade was opened.

The situation described in each of the bullets above are positive outcomes. You would have missed out on potential stock price upside that could occur above your strike price, but you would realize gains in the range of $9,165, or $16,185 or $286,177, not a loss.

In stark contrast, when you submit an order to sell to open 13 Eaton Calls with a $250 strike price and 56 days-to-expiration (a March 15, 2024, expiration date), you will see the "Max Loss" listed as, "Unlimited" (refer to the area circled in red in the message above). Making a trade that has an unlimited loss sounds scary, but the order is misleading. When I saw that the first time, it made me stop, and I did not submit the order until I had it clarified.

Turns out, the reason the order above states your max loss is unlimited is because the broker's platform assumes that you will intervene and pay to close the trade prior to the expiry date, instead of allowing the cover shares to be sold at the strike price. The trading platform assumes you will avoid assignments. In theory, the stock price could go to infinity, so in theory, how much you must pay to close prior to expiry is unlimited. With SUPER-CPT, you would not buy to close prior to expiry if doing so was unprofitable; you would simply allow the Calls to expire in-the-money, shares would be assigned (sold at the strike price), and you would realize large gains, not unlimited losses. You may miss out on some stock price upside that could occur beyond the price you sold the shares (strike price), but that is not a loss.

Active traders using margin will seldom allow trades to reach expiration, but with SUPER-CPT, you will not use margin so you should trade much differently than people who use margin. You can, and should, use your decision to not use margin to your advantage, but how to do that is simply not taught, or at the very least, it is difficult to find.

Your willingness to hold shares for an extended period—when you need to allow the stock price time to recover while the intrinsic value of the underlying business continues to grow—is another huge edge you will have when using SUPER-CPT. Active traders avoid assignments in general, and when put assignments happen and they buy the shares, they will seldom hold shares for an extended period. SUPER-CPT takes advantage of time and market volatility to avoid risking capital losses as well as avoids cash losses from closed trades. With SUPER-CPT, if you cannot select an acceptable strike price with short duration contacts, you will select a strike price from contracts further out in time. Higher strike prices will be available further out due to the combination of market volatility and time. The annualized returns will be lower for longer duration contacts than they would be for shorter duration contracts, but you still collect positive premiums and the returns are often still acceptable. By selecting a strike price high enough, at or above your assignment costs for the covered shares, there will be no risk of realizing a capital loss, and with no risk of a capital loss, you can abide the market and decide to have each trade closed profitably.

WHY ISN'T EVERYONE USING A SUPER-CPT SELLING OPTIONS STRATEGY?

So why isn't everyone selling options with a SUPER-CPT methodology? The five screens mentioned earlier probably filters out most people. To use SUPER-CPT successfully, you should have the required capital, invest in individual stock names, be comfortable with a buy-and-hold stock investing methodology, possess awareness of and have non-margin experience with stock options. Only a very few people will pass through all five requirements.

There is also a sixth reason, and it is a biggie. The brokerages make more profits when you trade options in the traditional manner, trying to predict near-term market movements, using margin, buying to open, avoiding assignments, trading more actively and so on. Even if brokers thought SUPER-CPT had merits, they would have no financial incentive to promote it to their clients (you).

How about you? Are you interested? Do I need to pull out the CAGR math again and create more graphs with higher CAGRs to illustrate the levels of wealth creation that are possible over decades?

I enjoy selling options, plus it has been financially rewarding, but you should make your own decision on whether to start selling options and with what strategy.

SUPER-CPT'S CAPITAL REQUIREMENTS

With SUPER-CPT, you will need enough money to avoid using leverage (no margin) and to allow you to have an adequate level of diversification within your portfolio of stocks and cash being used to sell options. Ideally, and this is only a rough rule of thumb, you should probably be able to dedicate a minimum of $500,000; this amount would allow you to hold some shares long plus sell both covered Calls and cash-secured Puts with eight different underlying stock names that have an average share price of about $185.

Most people sell options with less than $500,000. I have helped someone start selling options with as little as $15,000 in 2023. Starting with only $15,000, and using SUPER-CPT, is proving to be doable, but it is more difficult with lower performance expectations than if he had more capital; his diversification is low, less than ideal, and he can only afford to have a very limited number of trades open at any one time. The good news is he is only 25 years old, gaining valuable experience, and his limited capital constraints should hopefully melt away as his savings and stock investing portfolio value grow over time.

If you can dedicate more than $500,000 to selling options, even better. There is not an upper limit in practical terms. With a larger portfolio, up to the tens of millions of dollars and beyond, you simply sell multiple Calls and Puts instead of single contracts on each underlying stock.

Let's define the seven elements of SUPER-CPT a bit further.

SELL TO OPEN OPTIONS

Many people buy to open options, but selling options is what you should do. Buying options can be a bit like buying a lottery ticket; modest capital is required and there are high potential rewards, but there's also a low probability of success. You could win big, even quite big, but you are very likely to lose. Buying a lottery ticket or gambling is not the approach you should rely on to create your wealth.

In contrast, selling to open an option trade does require more capital, but it has a higher chance of success than buying to open an option trade. Sellers (you) earn the premium upfront and select strike prices that are unlikely to expire in the money, allowing the bulk of their trades to expire "out of the money." This allows you to use the same stock or cash to sell options again, earn even more premiums, and continue to repeat the process.

Selling options is like selling lottery tickets: you need lots of capital to do it, but the probabilities are on your side, and you should make fairly regular profits over time. Another analogy would be that you should sell to open stock options like good insurance companies sell insurance—preserve the value of your capital being used to secure contracts by having the probabilities on your side and collect generous and frequent premiums.

DO NOT USE MARGIN

"My partner Charlie says there are only three ways a smart person can go broke: liquor, ladies, and leverage,' Buffett explains, with 'leverage' referring to the practice of borrowing money to buy stocks. 'Now the truth is the first two he just added because they started with 'L'— it's leverage."
— WARREN BUFFETT

Many option traders use margin, also called leverage or debt, money borrowed from their stockbroker. You should not use margin because it comes with added cost and higher risks. The effect of not using margin is you will only be able to sell covered Calls or cash secured Puts, which means you will need to have sufficient stock or cash in your account for the option duration to sell or purchase the stock should the buyer of the Calls or Puts exercise his right to "call" or "put" the shares from or to you. Someone that uses margin would only have to keep a portion of the cash or a portion of the value of stock, not the full amount, in the account and their broker would eagerly lend them, for a fee, any additional amounts necessary.

Cash secured Puts and covered Calls have no margin requirement since the underlying stock or sufficient cash is already in the same account and will be used as the collateral for the open option contracts. You should not use leverage (debt or margin) when selling options. Only sell Calls on stocks that you already own and only sell Puts if you have sufficient cash in the same account to secure the Puts.

STAY UNCERTAIN ABOUT NEAR-TERM STOCK PRICE MOVEMENTS

"...fools and fanatics are so certain of themselves,
and wiser people are so full of doubts."
— BERTRAND RUSSELL

Many option traders spend time and effort trying to predict future short-term stock price movements. They use what is labeled as "Technical Analysis", although some critics derisively refer to Technical Analysis as Technical Astrology. Technical Analysis is an example of the types of esoteric aspects that can accompany complex topics. Technical analysts do not attempt to measure a stock's intrinsic business value, but instead, use stock charts to identify historical patterns and trends that they believe will enable them to accurately predict what a stock will do in the near-term. Many trading options training courses spend a lot of time teaching Technical Analysis. Practitioners diligently monitor historical and current market movements looking for patterns to find trading opportunities.

Most options are very short-term, typically less than 60 days-to-expiration. Even if your hunch should turn out to be accurate, if your prediction occurs after the expiry date you will still lose. If you believe you see historical patterns that will indicate the market's short-term future direction and act in accordance with those hunches, you will likely have random results over time.

I experimented with Technical Analysis decades ago. I found the process to be tedious, and when you considered all my outcomes, it yielded random results. Of course, someone could cherry-pick a portion of outcomes from Technical Analysis that were very good, but it is the overall results from all outcomes that matter when the goal is to build your wealth.

Trying to predict a stock's near-term future price movement is not just a waste of time. It can make an investor too confident about a predicted direction, impairing their overall performance. Instead, you should spend that time thinking through the possible future scenarios and only sell options when you have acceptable responses for each possible scenario.

"Therein lies a lesson in life. I think most lives work best when you simply react intelligently to the opportunities and difficulties you encounter, and just take the results as they fall."
— CHARLIE MUNGER

If you recall a prior section of *Wealthy & Wise*, you may notice that Technical Analysis is counter to Ben Graham's recommendation: an investor should not look to Mr. Market for advice. Technical Analysis looks right to the market for advice and is totally different from Ben Graham's approach to the market.

Humans tend to see patterns even in random data. We are wired to find patterns, to see meaning, but it's a glitch in our biological software. Frankly, I do not believe anyone can consistently predict short-term stock market movements over an extended period of time. Warren Buffett shares that view and has commented that the market-timers "Hall of Fame" is an empty room. Some things are just unpredictable.

"People have always had this craving to have someone tell them the future. Long ago, kings would hire people to read sheep guts. There's always been a market for people who pretend to know the future. Listening to today's forecasters is just as crazy as when the king hired the guy to look at the sheep guts."
— CHARLIE MUNGER

In contrast to Technical Analysis, fundamental analysis, such as Ben Graham's approach, that was covered in a prior section, has proven to be useful in determining long-term (but not short-term) price movements, and has enabled investors, like Warren, Charlie, Ben Graham, Peter Lynch, and others to create wealth.

With SUPER-CPT, you accept that you cannot accurately predict near-term stock price movements and do not waste your time trying to do so. Take some comfort from the fact that by not trying to predict the short-term market you will be in very good company with the likes of Newton, Buffett, Munger, and probably every successful stock investor with extensive investing experience. Stock prices will follow business performance, good or bad, over the long term but almost anything can, and does, happen to stock prices in the near term.

With SUPER-CPT, you will frequently sell both Calls and Puts on the same stock and have them both open at the same time. When the implied volatility is high enough, you can select large differences in the strike prices. If you select Call and Put strike prices with low Deltas, the most likely case is the stock price will remain within the range of the strike prices, below the Calls strike but above the Puts strike, and you will collect double premiums.

Below is an example of selling to open both Calls and Puts at the same time on the same stock with the same expiration, selecting the initial strike prices for the Calls and Puts with the same delta (the same probability of being assigned). In the options world, this is called a short strangle. The trade starts in a market neutral position and can realize profits, regardless of the stock price's unpredictable near-term movements:

- Tesla's stock price was $213.66 per share on June 6, 2023. I sold 30 Calls and 30 Puts on the same stock with the same days-to-expiration (10 days) and selected initial strike prices for the Calls ($230 per share) and Puts ($206.67 per share) with the same 25% probability of being assigned (a delta of 0.25). The Calls' cover shares had an assignment cost of $215 per share.

- I collected premiums of $15,960 ($8,280 for the Calls and $7,680 for the Puts) for the 10-day obligation on an at-risk value of $1,260,990. This yields a compound annual growth rate of 46% (15,960 divided by 10 days multiplied by 365 days is an annualized gain of 582,540. and then divided by the $1,260,990 value at risk).

- Possible outcomes on or before expiry:
  a. Most likely was stock price would stay within the range of the two strike prices, both options would expire worthless, and you would keep the full premium amount of $15,960 without having to sell or purchase any shares. Total gains for this scenario would be $15,960. You could then do a similar trade again, only ten days later, to collect more premiums.
  b. An alternative scenario is that the stock rises to above the Calls' strike price, you would allow the Calls to expire in-the-money, the shares would be assigned (sold at the strike of $230 per share) for a price higher than the stock price ($213.66 per share) was when

the Calls were opened and higher than the assignment cost ($215 per share) of the cover shares. Total gains would be $64,980: you would keep the $8,280 from Call premiums, plus capture a stock gain of $49,020 (shares sold for $230 strike price minus the $213.66 stock price when the calls were opened multiplied by 3,000 shares), plus the Puts would expire worthless, allowing you to keep the premium of $7,680 collected at open. Your cash position would have increased from selling the shares as well as collecting the premiums. You could then use your increased cash position to sell new Puts, only ten days later, to collect more premiums.

c.   The other possible scenario is the stock falls below the Puts' strike price during the contract duration. You keep the premiums collected of $15,960 and would allow the Puts to expire in-the-money. Puts would be assigned, and you would purchase the shares at $206.67 per share using the cash you set aside when you sold to open the Puts. You would then have double the number of shares and could use those shares to sell new Calls, only ten days later, and collect more premiums.

PROTECT EQUITY RISKED

The fourth key element of SUPER-CPT is to avoid realizing capital losses. Too many of the widely taught options trading strategies focus on premiums collected and mistakenly ignore the potential for, or even the realization of, capital losses. You realize a capital loss when you sell stock at prices below the price you paid to purchase those same shares. A stock loss only becomes a realized loss after you sell the shares.

Strike price management is key to protecting the value of your underlying stocks (equity). You should generally select a 30-to-60-day contract duration if you can select an acceptable strike price, but you will select longer durations if it is necessary to find a strike price that is above assignment cost. Shorter option durations, when they can be repeated continuously, will have better annualized returns than longer durations, but be patient when necessary to avoid risking capital losses. Avoiding the potential for capital losses will be worth the wait. Select longer Call durations when necessary to select a strike price high enough to be at or above the assignment cost of shares used to cover Calls.

The main risk occurs when the stock price plunges. When the stock price moves in a big way to well below your Puts' strike price, you will then buy the shares at an unrealized loss when the Puts are assigned. When the stock price has fallen a lot, once you buy the assigned shares you may not be able to select a short duration Call strike price that is above your assignment cost. Many people will simply sell Calls with a strike price below assignment cost and risk a capital loss, but that is not recommended if you are using SUPER-CPT. Instead, you should do the following:

- Consider longer duration contracts to see if you can find a Call strike price that is above your assignment cost (the annualized returns will be lower for longer duration contacts than they would be for shorter duration contracts, but you still collect positive premiums, the returns are often still good, and it allows you to avoid the risk of a capital loss).

- Or you can pause selling Call options with this stock until the stock price recovers. You are not collecting premiums during the paused period, but you avoid the risk of a capital loss. Using SUPER-CPT, you want to own the stock so you should not mind holding it.

You should not consider selling options on stocks that you do not want to have in your portfolio. When you can't find an acceptable call strike price that is greater than the assignment cost, you may need to pause selling options while the stock price recovers, meaning you will hold the stock. You will need the stock price to recover at some point, but recovery can take a long time. The stock could sit in your portfolio for a while, and you do not want to be forced to hold a position you hate. That's why you should only sell options on good businesses that you want to own.

If you realize capital losses, you will destroy some of the portfolio value that is being used to cover or secure your option trades. Frequent capital losses will rapidly diminish your wealth. You want to grow your wealth and therefore you want to avoid realizing capital losses when selling options.

If you do realize a capital loss, ensure you include the value impairment in your selling options performance reports.

Let's look at an actual example using PubMatic to highlight the benefits of being patient and extending durations to allow you to select strike prices above the assignment cost, so that you avoid realizing any cash or capital losses and end up with good overall returns.

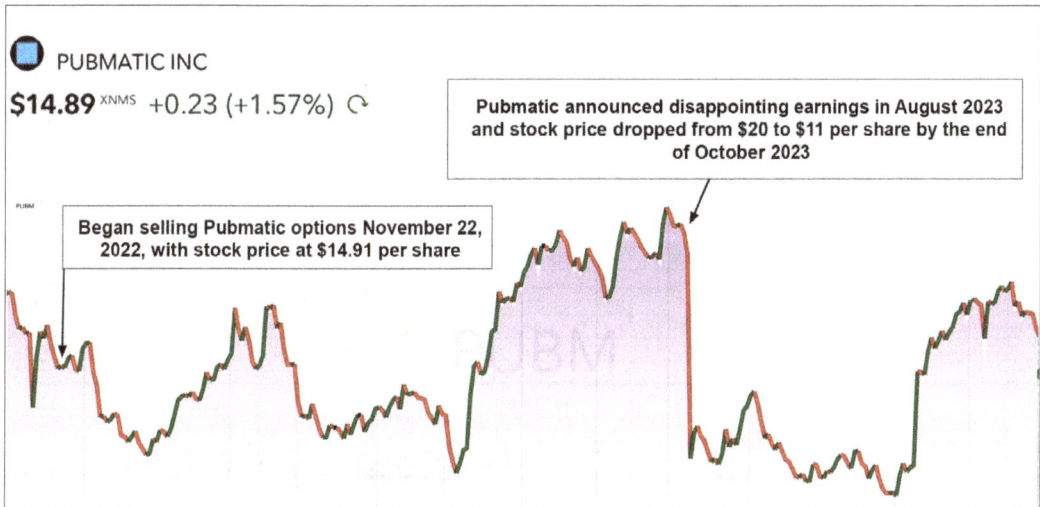

PUBMATIC INC
$14.89 XNMS +0.23 (+1.57%) ⟳

Pubmatic announced disappointing earnings in August 2023 and stock price dropped from $20 to $11 per share by the end of October 2023

Began selling Pubmatic options November 22, 2022, with stock price at $14.91 per share

PubMatic is a very small company, a micro-cap, and was added as an experiment to gain some experience selling options with a micro-cap. PubMatic is a solid business and their industry (digital advertising) was in a big slump in 2023 and may stay in the slump for a while. PubMatic has no debt, lots of cash, still generates free cash flow each quarter, so it should survive most possible industry downturns and be well positioned when the headwinds become tailwinds. PubMatic is not part of the buy-and-hold collection since there is not enough confidence yet that they can become a long-term compounding machine.

	Dates		Stock Price		Contracts			Premiums (per share)		Duration (Days)		Net Premiums at Close		
Trade Sets	Opened Trade	Closed Trade	At Open	At Close	Type	Number	Expiration Date	Strike Price	Open	Close	Open	Close	Gains or Loss ($)	Annualized ($)	Annualized (%)

Pubmatic (PUBM) - Option Contracts Opened in 2022 and 2023

Trade Sets	Opened Trade	Closed Trade	At Open	At Close	Type	Number	Expiration Date	Strike Price	Open	Close	Open	Close	Gains or Loss ($)	Annualized ($)	Annualized (%)
1	22-Nov-22	6-Jan-23	$14.91	$13.29	Puts	112	20-Jan-23	$12.50	0.55	(0.34)	59	45	$2,337	$18,959	13.77%
2	23-Nov-22	20-Jan-23	$15.45	$14.40	Puts	110	20-Jan-23	$15.00	1.20		58	58	$13,202	$83,083	54.73%
3	9-Jan-23	2-Feb-23	$13.74	$16.58	Puts	50	17-Feb-23	$12.50	0.58	(0.10)	39	24	$2,400	$36,500	60.73%
4	9-Jan-23	21-Apr-23	$13.82	$14.44	Puts	70	21-Apr-23	$12.50	1.18		102	102	$8,260	$29,558	37.30%
5	23-Jan-23	17-Feb-23	$14.60	$16.12	Calls	110	17-Feb-23	$15.00	0.60		25	25	$6,600	$96,360	62.57%
6	2-Feb-23	17-Mar-23	$16.74	$13.50	Puts	40	17-Mar-23	$15.00	0.71		43	43	$2,840	$24,107	42.17%
7	21-Feb-23	16-Mar-23	$16.17	$13.50	Puts	110	17-Mar-23	$15.00	0.75		24	23	$8,250	$130,924	83.52%
8	16-Mar-23	21-Apr-23	$13.50	$14.00	Calls	150	21-Apr-23	$15.00	0.30		36	36	$4,561	$46,245	23.36%
9	24-Apr-23	19-May-23	$14.00	$16.26	Calls	150	19-May-23	$15.00	0.46		25	25	$6,961	$101,631	50.05%
10	24-Apr-23	11-May-23	$14.44	$15.07	Puts	70	19-May-23	$12.50	0.35	(0.03)	25	17	$2,240	$48,094	56.41%
11	18-May-23	1-Jun-23	$15.84	$18.20	Puts	90	16-Jun-23	$15.00	0.42	(0.05)	29	14	$3,320	$86,560	65.73%
12	24-May-23	12-Jul-23	$17.35	$18.78	Puts	130	21-Jul-23	$17.50	1.30	(0.15)	58	49	$14,885	$110,878	52.15%
13	1-Jun-23	13-Jul-23	$18.20	$19.39	Puts	95	21-Jul-23	$17.50	0.88	(0.07)	50	42	$7,695	$66,873	42.18%
14	10-Jul-23	13-Jul-23	$17.57	$19.48	Puts	100	18-Aug-23	$17.50	1.19	(0.58)	39	3	$6,100	$742,167	439.41%
15	12-Jul-23	18-Aug-23	$18.75	$12.29	Puts	130	18-Aug-23	$17.50	0.70		37	37	$9,100	$89,770	41.10%
16	13-Jul-23	10-Aug-23	$19.46	$12.29	Puts	95	18-Aug-23	$17.50	0.53		36	28	$5,035	$65,635	40.71%
17	13-Jul-23	9-Aug-23	$19.58	$13.61	Calls	100	18-Aug-23	$20.00	1.14	(0.02)	36	27	$11,240	$151,948	82.33%
18	9-Aug-23	19-Jan-24	$13.61		Calls	100	19-Jan-24	$20.00	0.42		163	163	$4,200	$9,405	7.13%
19	10-Aug-23	19-Jan-24	$13.05		Calls	204	19-Jan-24	$17.50	0.68		162	162	$13,872	$31,255	12.39%
20	21-Aug-23	19-Jan-24	$12.31		Calls	21	19-Jan-24	$17.50	0.40		151	151	$840	$2,030	8.12%

Current Date:	31-Dec-23	$16.31		Total Net Premiums Collected During The Duration:	$133,939	$121,009	41.45%
Total Duration:	404		Contracts Open:	325		
				Average value of cash and stock at risk selling PUBM options:	$291,940	

In August 2023, PubMatic earnings disappointed and the stock price dropped a lot—from $20 at the end of August 2023 to $11 per share at the end of October 2023. PubMatic's 3Q earnings were better in November 2023 and the stock largely recovered and was above $16 per share at year-end 2023.

The SUPER-CPT test started selling options with PubMatic in November 2022. Above is a simplified tracker with each Pubmatic trade that was opened from the start (November 2022) through year-end 2023. Seventeen option trades, with multiple contracts for each trade, had been closed, and three trades were open at year-end 2023. Net premiums of $133,939 were collected, over thirteen months, using an average value at risk of $291,940.

No unprofitable trades were closed (net premiums for each of the 17 closed trades were positive), nor were any capital losses realized with PubMatic.

Pubmatic Cumulative Premiums Collected

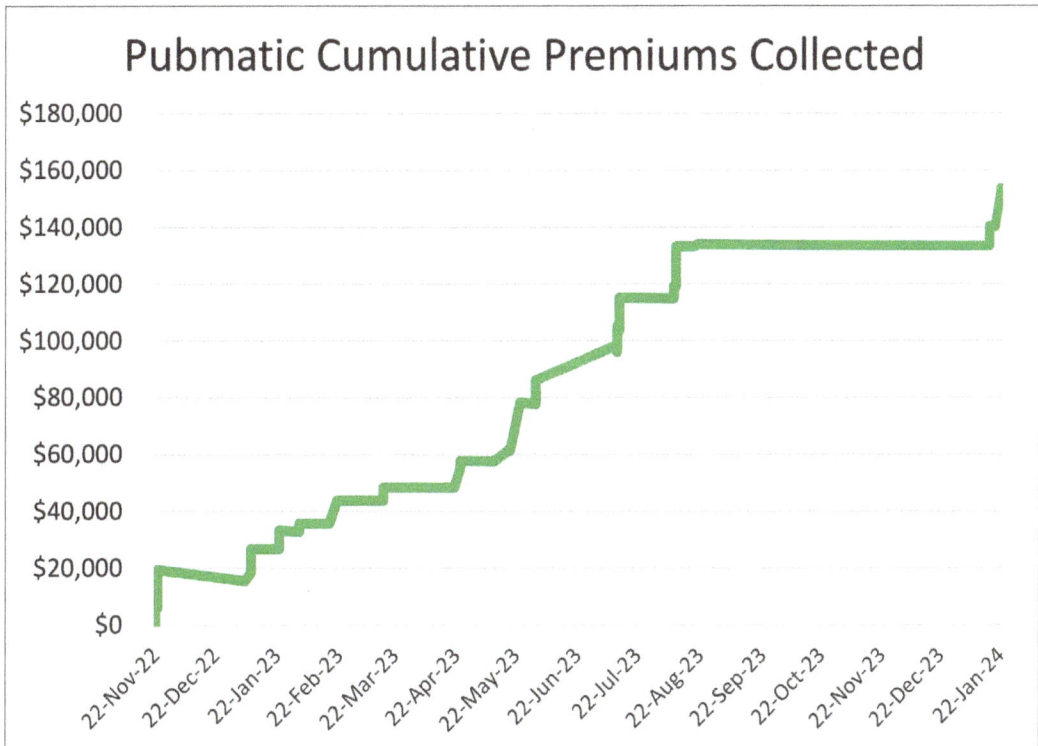

The compound annual growth rates from premiums were above 60% from the start in November 2022 through August 2023 (not shown in the table). That fell to 41% by year-end 2023 (shown in the bottom right of the table) because the sharp drop in stock price required extending durations out to January 19, 2024 on trades opened after the disappointing August earnings. Note in the table the last three trades have longer durations and the annualized returns are lower. The longer durations were necessary in order to find a strike price that was high enough above the depressed stock price to avoid the risk of realizing a capital loss. The annualized returns for the last three trades were 7, 12, and 8%. Lower than the average for the rest but still profitable and it avoided the risk of realizing a capital loss.

The good news is that allowing the in-the-money Puts to expire in August ensured the trade closed profitably, without realizing any cash losses from buying to close trades at a loss. Then, selecting longer durations for the new Calls avoided capital losses by selecting Call strike prices above the assignment costs. Selling options with more lucrative premiums has resumed now that the stock price has largely recovered.

When selling options, the good times can be so lucrative (60% CAGRs for PubMatic as of August 2023) that, if you avoid losses during bad times (when a stock price drops well below your assignment cost), your overall results (41% CAGRs as of year-end 2023) can still be excellent.

CLOSE PROFITABLE TRADES

Closing unprofitable trades is very common in the options world. Many active traders are willing to select strike prices that are below assignment costs, hoping the stock price stays below the Calls selected strike price. If the stock price behaves counter to what they hoped and rises above the strike price, they pay to close an unprofitable trade (a certain loss) and then sell to open a new one, hoping for an uncertain profit. With SUPER-CPT, you would select a strike price above assignment costs even if that required selecting options with more days-to-expiration.

Your notes allow you to plan and that planning helps you avoid emotional decisions later in the heat of the moment. Review and update the notes over time as you hold and before you sell an investment. Reading your writing will ensure your investment rationale and plans return to your inner voice's dialogue. Your writing will help to ensure that your Higher Mind is predominant, supporting your efforts to be rational when making investment decisions.

WRAP UP: HOW TO STAY RATIONAL WHEN MAKING INVESTMENT DECISIONS

A summary and suggestions:

- The conversation you listen to most often is not someone else speaking but instead you listen to the little voice in your own head.

- If you want to know someone has listened to your ideas, have them first read your ideas in writing, instead of only discussing it. Writing puts your voice in the reader's head.

- Writing also changes the writer. Sparks thinking and clarifies it.

- The inner voice concept is much, much bigger than just a life hack for getting people to listen to your proposals.
  - Our behavior, actions, and results are also consistent with the little voice in our head.

- ○ Our thought processes are dominated by having unspoken conversations with ourselves.
- ○ The inner voice is central to how we learn to control ourselves, and it shapes our wellbeing.

- Humans have a strange method for processing information that was initially controversial but is well established now.
  - ○ We have two simultaneous operating systems for processing information within our brains. It is like we have two minds in a single brain, and they are often in conflict.
  - ○ An Instinctual Mind: Is powerful, fast, intuitive, and creates instantaneous judgments that are most often our brain's default setting but it is prone to biases and is simply not designed to manage long-term risks over decades.
  - ○ A Higher Mind: Is a self-reflective consciousness that is rational, reasonable, and thoughtful but is slower, more analytical and using it for extended periods can be exhausting.
  - ○ Both, Instinctual and Higher, minds run simultaneously on your brain.

- Learning to think long-term and to control your emotions are crucial to successfully investing in stocks. You want your Higher Mind, not your Instinctual Mind, to be predominant when investing in stocks.

- The Instinctual Mind reacts rapidly and mostly below the level of our consciousness, but at times, especially stressful times, our Instinctual

Mind can dominate our inner voice.

- With effort, your Higher Mind can override or withstand the instincts, needs, or feelings your inner voice receives from your Instinctual Mind, and your overall wellbeing can benefit.

- Being able to place your Higher Mind in the driver's seat of your being is a volitional act—it's a learned skill.

- Stock investing provides incentives and countless opportunities to exercise and strengthen your mental powers of reasoning, imagination, and empathy, creating a more efficient and effective Higher Mind.

- To successfully invest, you need to win the struggle between the Instinctual Mind's impulsivity and the Higher Mind's self-control.

- Writing, 'perhaps the greatest of human inventions', can facilitate your effort to maintain self-control and stay rational when making investment decisions.
  - Create a habit of writing notes when you decide to buy a stock that include the gist of your analysis, possible future scenarios, and your plans for each.
  - Your notes allow you to plan and that planning helps you avoid emotional decisions later in the heat of the moment.
  - Review and update your investment notes over time as you hold and before you sell an investment.

- Reading your written notes will ensure your investment rationale and plans return to your inner voice's dialogue, and it will help to ensure that your Higher Mind is predominant and that you are rational when making investment decisions.

The reason unprofitability is so common is because most option traders use margin. Traders using margin want to avoid being assigned because that will require utilizing their expensive and risky margin. To avoid being assigned, they will buy to close open trades when or before they become in-the-money, paying more in premiums than they collected when they opened the trade. Those closed trades that have negative net premiums are unprofitable trades, and the cash losses add up. Those cash losses can become large cash losses that will impair your overall performance results. Those other strategies play a numbers game in the hope that a slightly larger percentage of profitable trades will outweigh many losers. You should avoid options strategies that involve numerous and frequent cash losses.

Below is a summary of an actual trade that resulted in negative net premiums (unprofitable) instead of positive net premiums (profitable). It was a mistake that occurred shortly after I began selling options and before I had developed the SUPER-CPT methodology:

- Berkshire has two classes of stock. The original shares are called A shares and later they introduced B shares that are worth 1/1,500 of an A share. Berkshire B shares are sometimes referred to as "Baby Berks." You cannot sell options with A shares, but you can with B shares. Berkshire Bs stock price was $312 per share on May 2, 2022.

- I sold to open 29 Calls, with a $322.50 strike price, 18 days-to-expiration, setting aside 2,900 shares to use as cover for the Calls, and collected $3.10 per share for a total premium of $8,990.

- The stock started to rise, reached $325 per share 3 days later. I irrationally changed my mind about the open trade, no longer wanting to sell stock at the $322.50 strike price, and decided to buy to close the position at a cost of $7.35 per share. The net premiums for the trade were negative. I collected $3.10 per share when the trade was opened but paid $7.35 per share to close the trade early for a net premium of -$4.25 per share or a total cash loss of $12,325.

- Instead of buying to close the trade early, one alternative would have been to allow the open trade to simply expire, 18 days after it was opened, and that would have eliminated having to pay any premium to close the trade. The net premiums for the trade would have been a profitable $3.10 per share ($3.10 to open and $0.00 to allow it to expire). The shares would have been sold if the stock price remained above the strike price, but that would have been additional profit when compared to the stock price when the Calls were opened.

You want to close profitable trades. When the sum of the premiums to open and close an options trade is a positive number, you create (realize) a cash gain and close a profitable trade. You want to avoid the inverse: closing unprofitable trades. When the sum of the premiums to open and close an options trade is a negative number, you paid more in premiums to "buy to close" the trade than you collected when you "sold to open" the trade. The net result creates a cash loss.

When using SUPER-CPT, you should be willing for shares to be assigned should the stock price move against you. Therefore, only sell to open Calls and Puts if you are willing to sell or buy the underlying shares. If that is unacceptable, adjust the strike price or do not sell those options. Be willing to allow assignments, to switch between Puts and Calls and to hold them until expiration.

AVOID OR MINIMIZE OTHER CASH LOSSES

With SUPER-CPT, you will avoid closing unprofitable trades. The other cash losses that should be avoided or minimized include taxes, margin interest, and other transactional costs. Plus, you should earn competitive interest rates on cash, and that includes on cash being used to secure Puts because from a competitive perspective it is financially equivalent to incurring cash losses if others do and you do not.

You should minimize taxes by doing your option trades in tax-free (a Roth IRA) or tax-deferred (traditional IRAs) accounts. When you sell options, the positive net premiums collected can generate high levels of income, plus you can realize capital gains as well. You will owe taxes on the selling options income and any realized capital gains if you trade options in a taxable account.

If you do use stocks in taxable accounts to sell options, avoid using stocks with large unrealized capital gains to avoid realizing capital gains in the event a Call's strike price is reached. (Remember the beneficial tax effect for buy and hold investing that was covered earlier?) For example, the Amazon shares, with unrealized gains (profits) at more than 99% of the current stock price, plus shares in some of my Berkshire Hathaway, Tesla, and other stock names with large unrealized gains are in a taxable account, and you would not use those shares to sell Call options to eliminate the risk of realizing capital gains now that can be deferred for a long time instead.

With SUPER-CPT, you will hold some shares long as well as sell options with other shares in the same stock name. Using your taxable accounts to hold shares long while selling options with those same underlying stocks in tax advantaged accounts is a best practice.

Options trading commission costs have decreased significantly in the last twenty years, and that has been a good thing for investors. Most brokerages now only charge minimal commissions per trade. While options trading's explicit costs have become close to zero, implied transaction costs from bid-ask spreads have not come down near as much, allowing market makers to still extract considerable fees from investors like you. Bid-ask spreads are narrow (efficient) in options with large liquidity. When bid-ask spreads are wide, use limit orders, instead of submitting market orders, to minimize the cost.

Here are a few other transactional costs that can be quite expensive—creating what is equivalent to large cash losses—and the investor should avoid or minimize them.

Margin interest is the fee charged for borrowing money from your brokerage firm. Brokerage's will charge margin interest when an investor wishes to use leverage (debt). With SUPER-CPT, you will avoid margin costs entirely since you will only sell Calls on stocks that you already own, and you only sell Puts if you have sufficient cash in the same account to secure the contracts.

A more indirect, perhaps hidden, cost that you want to avoid is that your brokerage will sometimes automatically establish a sub-optimal money market cash position for you when you open an account. The money market is primarily used for processing cash transactions and for holding uninvested cash. There are usually alternative cash positions available that would pay higher interest than the one the broker automatically provides to you. You should ask your brokerage about alternative money market cash positions and compare the interest rates. I have helped friends select very safe cash positions that pay higher interest than their initial default money market position.

Finally, some brokers allow you to earn interest, currently at 5%, on cash when you are using that cash to secure open Puts. However, some 'zero-commission' and perhaps other brokerages do not pay you interest on cash that is being used to secure Puts. With SUPER-CPT, a large portion of your trades will be cash-secured Puts. Earning 5% on that cash is a huge edge and would be equivalent to a large cash loss if you used a brokerage that did not pay interest on cash being used to secure Puts.

Track Results

> *"Everything is vague to a degree you do not realize*
> *till you have tried to make it precise."*
> — BERTRAND RUSSELL

You need to keep track of your results and document your learnings from selling options. Track your results for each transaction and cumulatively over time for each stock name being used to sell options.

You should track actual results in a spreadsheet with details of each decision. Document any actions that deviated from your strategy. Doing this will accelerate learning. Your tracker should include each option trade you make, good or bad, to ensure accuracy and utility.

You will need to track the assignment cost of your covered shares. Assignment cost excludes any benefits to the cost or sales basis from premiums collected since, with SUPER-CPT, you will account for premiums separately when tracking performance.

You also should ensure your reported gains account for outcomes when Call strike prices were reached at expirations that result in capital losses or gains. If you only account for premium outcomes in your options' performance results, instead of both premium and strike price outcomes, your results will be incomplete, and you will be incentivized to set strike prices too aggressively. You do not want to be incentivized to buy stocks at high prices and sell stocks at lower prices, but you will be if you only look at premiums and neglect strike price outcomes.

Track your net premiums collected from closed trades plus any realized capital gains or losses and any dividends collected. Include all three in selling options performance results.

You should set goals, a return target for selling options, and track your actual results versus your goals. For example, as already mentioned, my return target for selling options is to earn at least a 20% CAGR on the total at-risk value (stocks and cash) being used to sell options. The return target can be met through a combination of collected net premiums, realized net capital gains, and collected dividends. SUPER-CPT actual test results from November 2022 through year end 2023 collected net premiums that yielded a 31% CAGR on the average value at risk (stocks and cash) being used to sell options, well above the 20% target for selling options. Unrealized gains and unrealized losses do not need to be tracked every time stock prices change, stock prices change too frequently, but should also be tracked periodically, at least annually.

It is useful to be reminded of, and even to dwell on, your mistakes. To do that, you kind of need to mentally rub your nose in them. You will make mistakes selling options and those losses, or less than optimal gains, should be included in your reported results.

SELLING OPTIONS FORWARD PLAN

I continue to be delighted with how lucrative and interesting selling options has been. I especially like that I can earn premiums even when stocks are flat or going down instead of only having gains in an up market. By selling options, you can generate income while waiting for the business to be weighed by a fickle stock market. My wealth was built without selling options, and my selling options experience is still in its early days. However, I believe a cautious combination of buy-and-hold investing plus selling options can result in higher returns than if you only currently do buy-and-hold investing. There is much more to learn, but the rewards have been well worth the effort. I learn best by doing, so I am glad I started and will continue to sell options with a portion of my stock investing portfolio.

Watch this space. If you are interested, I will provide an update on my selling options results in future editions of *Wealthy & Wise*, and I am willing to keep you informed as I gain more experience.

WRAP-UP: SELLING STOCK OPTIONS

A summary list and suggestions:

- Selling options will seem difficult at first, but most things seem difficult at first.

- The reason to bother selling options at all is because it can be lucrative enough to improve your stock investing financial performance.

  o You can generate income from assets (stocks or cash) that you already own by collecting premiums each time you sell to open an option contract.

  o Selling options can also allow you to sell shares that you already own at a higher than current market price and it can allow you to purchase shares of stock at a lower than current market price.

  o Actual results for all option trades are an overall 30% CAGR thus far, exceeding the target of 20% CAGR by a large margin. It has been 639 days through year-end 2023 since selling options began, less than 2 years. Results will continue to be tracked.

- The world of stock options can be risky and complex. You will want to understand what matters and follow a well-defined strategy for selling options.

- When you want to learn complex topics, understand how and why they work, "invert, always invert."

- **SUPER-CPT** selling options strategy (**S**tay **U**ncertain, **P**rotect **E**quity **R**isked, and **C**lose **P**rofitable **T**rades) only sells covered call and cash-secured put options with stocks you own, or want to own for the long-term, selects strike prices at or above assignment cost to avoid realizing capital losses, collects positive net premiums on each trade, and it does all that without you having to be able to predict near-term stock price movements. The following seven elements are foundational to the strategy:

1. Sell to open options. Do not buy to open.

2. Do not use margin. Only sell covered Calls and/or cash secured Puts.

3. Stay Uncertain about future near-term stock price movements. Do not try to predict near-term market direction. Sell to open an options trade only when all scenarios are acceptable.

4. Protect Equity Risked. To avoid realizing capital losses, select Call strike prices that are at or above the assignment cost (or at or above the cost basis when shares were purchased directly) for the shares being used to cover the Calls.

5. Close Profitable Trades. Buy to close early, prior to expiry, only when the cost to close is less than the amount collected when opened, otherwise allow open contracts to expire and accept assignments if they occur.

6. Avoid or minimize other cash losses. Sell options in tax advantaged accounts, avoid margin interest, earn competitive interest rates on cash and on cash being used to secure Puts, and minimize other transactional costs.

7. Track results. Keep sufficient records to enable accurate performance monitoring.

- Utilizing SUPER-CPT will greatly simplify what you need to learn about options trading since much of what happens in the options trading world is now no longer relevant if you do not use margin, do not try to predict near-term stock price movements, do not buy to open, and are willing to accept assignments. The complex and risky options world is greatly reduced to a simpler, safer subset of activities.

- Only sell options on stocks that you already own or want to own, stocks of good businesses that you believe will continue to grow their intrinsic business value over the long-term and that you are willing to hold for as long as they remain good businesses. Stock selection methodology is therefore the same as what was already covered for buy-and-hold investments.

- Once open contracts are closed early, or expire, you use the same stock or cash to cover or secure the "sell to open" of new options again and collect more premiums, repeatedly, for as long as you can continue to find acceptable strike prices.

- Your primary objectives using SUPER-CPT are...
  1. to protect the value of capital (also called equity or stocks) at risk that is being used to cover call option contracts by selecting Call strike prices that are at or above the assignment cost for the shares being used to cover the Calls (or at or above the cost basis when cover shares were purchased directly);
  2. only buy to close a trade early if the cost to close is less than the amount collected when it was opened, otherwise allow open contracts to expire and accept any assignments if they occur;

3. then, only after satisfying the first two objectives, maximize the annualized returns from net premiums collected by repeatedly selling option contracts, earning premiums each time trades are closed, to maximize the annualized returns on the value at risk dedicated to selling options.

- You will love collecting premiums, but you will not enjoy giving up completely on stock price gains that may occur beyond a Calls' strike price and you also will not want to lose all of your shares. You should therefore hold some shares long, shares that are not used to cover Calls, to ensure that you will participate at least partially in any stock price gains that may occur beyond the selected Call strike prices should there be a large, rapid gain in stock price.

- In a discrete worst possible case, a very large stock price drop that goes well below your Puts' strike price, SUPER-CPT's forward outlook will have the same risks as a buy-and-hold investment. In all other cases, with SUPER-CPT you are collecting positive net premiums but giving up some potential stock price upside versus buy-and-hold investing.

- Results from the conservative strategy, SUPER-CPT, have exceeded expectations. Results from November 2022 through year end 2023 collected net premiums that yielded a 31% CAGR on the average value at risk (cash or stock value) being used to sell options. The 31% CAGR earned with SUPER-CPT is well above the 20% target for selling options.

- Unlike SUPER-CPT, strategies that use margin will seldom allow trades to reach expiration and will avoid assignments. Doing both necessitates closing a lot of unprofitable trades when the amount paid to close a trade exceeds the amount you collected to open the trade.

- With SUPER-CPT you will not use margin, so you should trade much differently than people that use margin. You can abide Mister Market's erratic near-term stock price movements and decide to have each closed trade be profitable, collecting positive net premiums without realizing any capital losses.

  ○ Selecting Call strike prices at or above assignment costs will avoid realizing capital losses.

  ○ Allowing open contracts to expire and accept assignments if they occur allows each closed trade to be profitable.

  ○ Your willingness to hold shares for an extended period, instead of risking capital losses and unprofitable trades when the stock price needs time to recover, creates a huge edge.

- What's the catch? Or why isn't everyone selling options with a SUPER-CPT methodology? Only a very few people will pass through the following six screens:

  1. Have the required capital,
  2. Invest in individual stock names,
  3. Be comfortable with a buy-and-hold stock investing methodology,
  4. Possess awareness of stock options, and

5. Have non-margin experience with stock options

6. Plus, a sixth reason, the brokerages make more profits when you trade options in the traditional manner, using technical analysis and margin, avoiding assignments, trading more actively and so on. Even if brokers thought SUPER-CPT had merits, there would be no financial incentives to promoting it.

- With SUPER-CPT, you will need enough money to avoid using leverage (no margin) and enough to allow you to have an adequate level of diversification within your portfolio of stocks and cash that you will use to sell options.

  ○ Ideally, and only a rough rule of thumb, you should probably be able to dedicate a minimum of $500,000 to selling options.

  ○ There is no upper limit in practical terms. With a larger portfolio, up to and beyond tens of millions of dollars, you simply sell multiple Calls and Puts instead of single contracts on each underlying stock.

CLOSING
REMARKS

———————

Wealthy & Wise was written because I want you to become financially independent and I was disappointed with the third-party resources that I could find about investing. I hope the content helps you become wealthy, but I also hope you will want more than just money.

"To get what you want, you have to deserve what you want. The world is not yet a crazy enough place to reward a whole bunch of undeserving people."
— CHARLIE MUNGER

Charlie often says that Warren "takes the high road. It's less crowded." You should take the high road too, even if taking the high road makes less money. The interesting thing is Warren and Charlie insist that, in fact, you make more money by taking the high road in business and in life. Charlie even says if criminals knew how well behaving credibly worked, they would change. Being transparent, ethical, and deserving of what you want is so rare; you will have fewer competitors. Decide that you will do what needs to be done to deserve what you want. That journey may be easier than you imagine, and you may just be pleasantly surprised.

> *"Two roads diverged in a wood, and I —*
> *I took the one less traveled by,*
> *And that has made all the difference."*
> —ROBERT FROST

Warren often tells a story when talking to students—he told it to my MIT class in the year 2000—about how they can use reason to determine their framework for ethics. For me, it also illustrates one of many conflicts (reason versus a self-serving bias) between our Higher and Instinctual Minds that you can, and need to, control.

Warren asks students, "Play a little game with me."

"Imagine that it is 24 hours before your birth and a genie comes to you with the following proposition:

'You look like a bright prospect,' the genie would say, 'I'm going to let you set the rules of the society in the world you will enter in 24 hours. You'll determine what the social, political, and economic rules will be. You are all-powerful, divine, and godly. You will make all the rules. That's going to be it.'

'What's the catch?' You'll want to know.

'The catch is that you don't know whether you're going to be male or female, rich or poor, able bodied or infirmed, black or white, born in the United States or Somalia, low or high intelligence, and so on.'

After you make your world, you must draw a ticket out of a barrel at random—Warren calls it the ovarian lottery. Basically, you will set the rules that will govern your life, but your life will be one out of 7 billion possible lives—7 billion possible tickets and you will be randomly assigned one of those tickets. Keep in mind that you have a less than 5% chance of being born in the United States, and an even less chance of being born into an American family that feels "fairly" financially secure.

"What kind of world would you want to emerge into when you don't know what ticket you're gonna get?" Buffett asked the students.

"What is a just world?" he asks. You should decide for yourself.

Warren admires people who would set rules that are not overly biased in favor of their own starting point. It's difficult and rare to do since humans have a self-serving bias (part of our Instinctual Mind's ancient survival software), thinking that what is good for them is good for the wider civilization. It is because of this bias that people can rationalize ridiculous conclusions based on a subconscious tendency to serve oneself.

Warren hopes the kind of world created would 1.) be such that it would allow talent to rise to the top (if you want the very highest reaches of civilization, you want to get responsibility into the hands of the people with the most talent and have them motivated enough that they want to work long after they have enough money to quit, to continue producing for the benefit of others) but 2.) he hopes the world created would also provide all with the chance to meet their full potential.

Through this game of 'pretend,' Warren hopes to help participants shift their perspectives on their own lives.

When you can remove your self-serving bias from your own thinking and conduct, and at the same time, allow for the self-serving bias in others who have not removed it yet, you become more rational and get a great advantage in life. Most people are not going to remove their bias successfully—the human condition being what it is. But when you can remove it in investing and beyond, you start to understand that investing, learning, this world, is not all just about us. There's more to it.

The Wealthy & Wise methodology is to buy stocks of good to wonderful businesses, don't overpay, and hold them for decades. You will become a collector, using a long-term, buy-and-hold stock investing strategy, and this approach has substantial advantages versus both mutual fund investments and more active stock investing strategies. The wealth differences after decades are huge and in favor of the buy-and-hold strategy. The behavioral habits you need are within reach:

- Develop a habit of spending less than you make so you can save money regularly to invest.
- Learn how to be rational, keep your emotions in check, and maintain self-control when you make investment decisions.

- Invest your savings as early, and as much, as you can. Start now.

- Learn to distinguish good from bad businesses since, in the long run (over decades), it is the quality of the business that you invested in which determines your returns.

- Own shares in a diversified collection. Your collection can be a small number, ten good businesses is enough, if diversified.

- Never interrupt compounding unnecessarily, stay invested through bull and bear markets, do not try to time the market, hold for decades.

You should not lose money overall if the stocks are held long enough. When you combine even modest savings with the habits above, you will unleash the magic of compounding and over long time periods you will create levels of wealth well beyond what you initially saved.

Once you have accumulated some wealth, you can also consider using a portion of your buy-and-hold portfolio to sell stock options using a low-risk strategy, like SUPER-CPT. For such a low-risk strategy, SUPER-CPT can be very lucrative and when combined with a buy-and-hold stock investing methodology can be more financially rewarding than if you only do buy-and-hold stock investing.

The power of Wealthy & Wise investing goes beyond the ability to make you wealthy. You become a learning machine, a lifelong learner. You stay engaged in ideas and aware of what is happening in the world. You enhance your ability to think independently and critically and strengthen your reasoning, imagination, and empathy. You invert, focus on what matters while tuning out noise and take advantage of market volatility. You anticipate trouble and perform adequately when trouble comes. You encourage your curiosity, collect the best ideas, and use them often so that they stay fresh. You sit with the discomfort of being bad while you learn. You embrace uncertainty, humility, and humor.

Overall, investing the Wealthy & Wise way allows you to explore the wonders of the world. Your explorations are interesting, lucrative, and fun. Your journey awaits. You should take the high road, the one less crowded, but you need to start. The sooner the better.

I hope some of the above material proves useful. Think about me now and then, and please keep in touch.

Best and warmest wishes,

David Chenier

www.ingramcontent.com/pod-product-compliance
Lightning Source LLC
Chambersburg PA
CBHW080758300326
41914CB00055B/934